CAST ALL YOUR ANXIETIES ON HIM,

because he cares for you.

I Peter 5:7

Who is Dr. Joy?

Dr. Joy Greene loves Jesus and her heartbeat centers around encouraging women through His Word. Her greatest callings in life are to be Bryan's wife and Ellie and Sam's mom. "Dr. Joy," as she is fondly called by those who know her is an author, professor, speaker, and radio personality.

Dr. Joy earned her doctorate degree in pharmacy and she is passionate about teaching student pharmacists. In addition to her career as a pharmacy professor, Joy is the founder of Joytime Ministries, a non-profit women's ministry where she encourages women with the hope of Jesus!

She hosts a nationally syndicated radio feature called "Joytime" that airs on radio stations across the world. She speaks nationally at women's events, and she connects daily with her Joytime online community through her social media accounts.

She and her team work with some of the nation's most dynamic worship leaders to host women's retreats. These weekend retreats bring women from all over the country together for a weekend of worship, encouragement, and fun!

You can listen to "Joytime" radio features, learn about Joytime events, visit the online Joytime Shop, and find godly encouragement at www.joytime.org.

You can find weekly encouragement and plug into Joytime online Bible studies by connecting with the Joytime Ministries Facebook page or on Instagram (@itsdrjoy).

A Prescription for Joy

OVERCOME WORRY WITH FIVE STEPS

Dr. Joy Greene

Joytime Ministries, Inc.
Dr. Joy Greene | @itsdrjoy | www.joytime.org

ISBN-979-8-9864723-2-4
Joytime Ministries Publishing

PUBLISHED IN THE UNITED STATES OF AMERICA

Contents

Introduction

It's Okay
TO FEEL

It's Okay to Feel
Introduction

Worry. It's a joy-stealer. It's a relationship-breaker. It's a life-thief. Throughout my life, I have been a worrier. There was a time when I deserved a sparkly crown and sash because I considered myself the Queen of Worry. I worried about so many things...big things, little things, silly things. I even worried about the fact that I worried too much. Maybe you have been there too.

My struggle with worry has caused me to lose sleep, eat too much or too little, cry, scream, have nervous energy, doubt God, and experience panic. The list goes on. What about you?

The fact that you decided to pick up this book leads me to believe that, like me, you have also struggled with worry. I wonder if you find yourself in an awful season of worry right now. Maybe it is spinning out of control, and you have no idea what to do. I understand. I've been there. I know how terrible it feels.

One thing I've learned about worry is it rarely invades your life without bringing its friends, Embarrassment, Shame, and Isolation along for the journey.

It is not uncommon to feel embarrassed when you struggle with worry. I do not know anyone who is proud of their struggles with worry, do you? Have you ever seen a t-shirt that reads, "Proud to be a Worrywart," or a bumper sticker that reads, "Honk if you love to worry!"?

Have you ever heard of an adorned superhero named "Worry Woman" who jumps to the worst conclusion in a single bound? Of course not. No one is proud that they struggle with worry. None of us shout it from our rooftops that we often feel overwhelmed with worry and fear. Instead, we feel ashamed and embarrassed. We often hide in the darkness we feel. We wonder why we don't have our lives all together like other people. We feel undone.

When we struggle with worry and fear, it is easy to slip into isolation and loneliness. We do not want others to know we are struggling, so we do our best to hide it. We make up excuses to skip social gatherings, and we prefer texting over talking on the phone in hopes no one will discover we are sinking in despair.

When I have struggled with worry, I believed the lie, "If I had more faith, I would never struggle with this." I also believed I was a failure because I could not get a handle on my excessive worrying. I wondered what was wrong with me. Why could I not just "snap out of it?" Maybe you have felt this way too. It encourages me when I remember worry is a feeling. It is only a feeling. It is important we understand our feelings.

God created us to feel. Worry is only a feeling.

Rewrite that sentence in the space below:

_____

_____

_____

We live in a culture that tells us something is wrong if we don't feel happy all the time. Think about the advertisements you see online and on television. Happy, smiling, beautiful people who have perfectly organized homes, and thin, fit bodies. I don't know about you, but

3

that does not describe my life.

I am not always happy. I do not always feel like smiling. My house looks lived-in, and my body is far from perfect. Feeling pressured to live a flawless life is a false perception of what real life is. It is also a false perception of who God created us to be. God made us emotional beings. He created us to FEEL. We have ups and downs, good days and bad days, victories, and failures. We are human, and we have feelings. It's okay for us to feel. God designed us that way.

In the book of Ecclesiastes, we read these words:

> *There is a time for everything, and a season for*
> *every activity under the heavens: a time to weep*
> *and a time to laugh, a time to mourn and*
> *a time to dance.*
> *~Ecclesiastes 3:1,4*

Experiencing a variety of emotions and feelings does not mean you are unstable. It does not mean your life is full of chaos. Experiencing a variety of emotions and feelings means you are human. Take your heart as an example. Have you ever been a patient in a hospital? If so, you may have had your heart monitored with an EKG test. When this test is used, electrodes are placed on your chest to monitor the electrical activity of your heart. The heart monitor of someone with normal electrical activity looks like this:

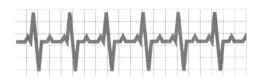

The up and down activity of this heart monitor shows there is a beating heart. It shows there is life!

On the flip side, when someone's heart stops beating, the electrical activity looks like this:

A flat line. No ups and downs. No activity. No life.

Highs and lows, ups and downs...this is what life is made of. When you and I experience feelings, it means we are alive. Feelings are a part of living. It's okay for you to feel. I want you to personally embrace this thought:

Feelings are a part of living. It's okay for me to feel.

Rewrite that statement below:

_____

_____

Jesus never modeled for us that feelings are wrong. The Bible shows us Jesus expressed many different feelings. He felt anger, distress, compassion, and sorrow. He groaned, cried, rejoiced, suffered and the list goes on. Through the pages of our Bibles, we see the perfect Son of God - feel. Jesus understands our emotions. He understands our feelings. This truth brings me a lot of comfort.

Feelings are not good or bad. Although they are an important part of who we are, we need to recognize that our feelings are not truth. Just because we feel a certain way does not mean it is reality. Our feelings will lie to us, and Satan will use our feelings against us. We need to be careful we do not let our feelings sit in the driver's seat of our life. If we do, we will be an emotional wreck waiting to happen.

Feelings have their place in our lives and as we give them over to God, He can help us learn to manage them in a healthy way. We do not always have a choice in how we feel, but we do have a choice in how we respond! Our feelings can drive us to fall apart, or they can drive us to fall at the feet of Jesus. This is true for our feelings of worry, too.

WORRY VERSUS CONCERN

Often, in the English language, the words worry and concern are used interchangeably, but they do not mean the exact same thing. Let's take a look at how they are different. Let's start with the word, concern. How do you define it? Write down your thoughts below:

_____

_____

_____

_____

Concern is a feeling that is mostly viewed as something positive. Feeling concerned shows we care deeply about someone or something. In the Bible, we read about godly concern. This type of concern is focused on the things of God. One place we see the expression of this type of godly concern is in the book of Philippians:

I have no one else like him, who will show genuine
concern for your welfare.
~Philippians 2:20

We also see godly concern expressed in the verse below from the book of 1 Corinthians:

An unmarried man is concerned about the Lord's
affairs—how he can please the Lord.
~1 Corinthians 7:32b

Having godly concern motivates us to do something good. It is a part of having godly character. On the flip side, there is another type of concern mentioned in the Bible. We often see it in scripture as our English word, "worry" and it is always referenced as something negative. When you think about the word, "worry," what comes to your mind? Write down your thoughts below:

_____

_____

_____

_____

Worry occurs when our feelings of concern become excessive. Thoughts about bad things that might happen cause us to be more focused on our problems and less focused on God. Worry can distract us from doing what God desires, and it can cause us to doubt the goodness of God. Worry overshadows the faithfulness of God as it causes us to dwell on negative things. We see this word used a few times in scripture:

But the Lord answered and said to her, "Martha, Martha,
you are worried and bothered about
so many things."
~Luke 10:41

7

Therefore I tell you, do not worry about your life,
what you will eat or drink; or about your body, what
you will wear. Is not life more than food, and the
body more than clothes?
~Matthew 6:25

When Jesus says, "Do not worry," He is not telling us to go through life being happy-go-lucky while ignoring the circumstances of our lives. Instead, He is explaining that the focus of our lives should not revolve around our problems. He wants us to trust in Him. He knows we will have concerns in life, but with the right perspective and by using scripture as our guide, feelings of concern do not have to spin out of control. We can trust that even when bad things happen, God has the power to work things together for something good.

And we know that God causes all things to work together
for good to those who love God, to those who are called
according to His purpose.
~Romans 8:28

Do you believe in your heart and mind that God can take all of your life's circumstances (even the bad ones) and use them for something good? Can you think of times in your life when you saw God do that? How has God worked something good from a bad situation?

What about worry? Do you believe God can even use your struggle with worry for something good? If you are unsure, then I want you to know with confidence, He can! When you give your struggle with worry over to God, He can turn it into something good. Take a moment and say this statement out loud to yourself: "God can use my struggle with worry for something good." Now, write that in the space below:

God can use my struggle with worry for something good.

_____

_____

You may be wondering, "How can God use something so detrimental as worry and fear for something good?" I understand how you could feel that way. I know firsthand how worry makes you feel trapped in a dark place. I know how it feels to believe there is no way out of that darkness, but my friend, you and I need to remember who our God is!

"I am the Lord, the God of all mankind.
Is anything too hard for me?"
~Jeremiah 32:27

We need to remember God is all-powerful. May we never forget how mighty He is. When I think about how He spoke this world into existence, I am reminded there is nothing too difficult for Him! God can take your struggle with worry and bring something beautiful from it. With His help, you can break the stronghold that worry has on your life!

Would you like to find a way to overcome your excessive worrying? Would you like to be free from the chains of worry? Would you like to throw off the huge weight of worry that hovers over your life and instead, live with more joy? If your answer is "yes" to those questions, I am so glad you picked up this book. You will find tools, strategies, and tips in this book that you can use to help you manage worry.

You are not alone in how you feel. I understand what it feels like to have worry rob your life of happiness and joy. I know what it feels like to walk through that dark place. I know what it feels like to wonder if you will ever get your life back. It is normal to have feelings of worry, but sometimes our feelings get the best of us. Sometimes we give them too much power in our lives. We can be encouraged by knowing God wants to help us manage our feelings. He wants to give us joy, peace, and freedom from the chains of worry.

In this book, I will give you five important steps that have helped me overcome the damaging effects of excessive worry in my life. You can begin using these practical steps right away in your life. They are simple, grounded in God's Word, and align with the medical literature. I will also provide strategies, tools, and tips I have found helpful to prevent worry from taking over my mind.

As a pharmacist, I have filled many prescriptions in my career. A prescription (Rx) is a recommendation that is given by someone in the medical field. It is a short list of things a patient needs to treat a condition. At the end of each section, a prescription graphic contains a list of important takeaway points from that section. These main points are items I encourage you to implement into your life. Think of each Rx as a list of action items you can put into practice to help you overcome your struggle with worry. Utilize these important, main points as you work your way through the book.

As you read each section, be careful not to rush. Take your time. You may want to read each section more than once. I have provided space for you to think and reflect along the way. I have also provided space at the end of each section for you to write down what main points encouraged you.

It will be helpful for you to have a journal as you begin this book. Throughout this book, I have provided journaling questions for you to consider. Having a journal will help you manage your worrisome thoughts and feelings.

I am so happy you are joining me on this journey! With God's help, you can find your way back to the life He wants you to live. With His help, you can find your way back to joy and peace. With His help, you can find your way out of the darkness.

I can't wait to get started!

~Dr. Joy

Step One

WORK THROUGH YOUR WORRY

FACE YOUR WORRY HEAD-ON

Step One: Work Through Your Worry

Have you ever stopped to think about how amazing the human body is? As a pharmacist, throughout my education and career, I have studied how the human body works and I am amazed at how God created our bodies in such an intricate way. The more I have studied the body through medicine, the more amazed I have been to know God as Creator. God designed our bodies with trillions of cells that not only heal themselves but also make new cells to replace ones that have been damaged. We are made in His image and His design is incredible.

Have you ever wondered what happens inside your body when you feel worried? Understanding how your body works can be empowering. During my journey in overcoming worry, having greater knowledge of how my body worked, helped me manage my feelings better. The more I understood how my body reacted to stress, the better I could respond mentally and emotionally. So, what happens inside your body when you feel worried? Let's dive into this by first examining the differences between three common terms: worry, stress, and anxiety.

Worry, stress, and anxiety are not the same. Although we sometimes use these terms interchangeably, they are different. Let's examine their differences.

WHAT IS WORRY?

Worry is when our minds dwell on negative things. Often, we dwell on things that could go wrong in our lives. The word "dwell" is important. Worry is more than just thinking briefly about something negative. Worry occurs when your mind sits in the negativity. It happens when your mind gets stuck on something negative.

Most everyone experiences worry from time to time. People often worry about one specific thing and the feeling of worry usually comes and goes. It is normal to feel worried about taking an important test. It is normal to feel worried about an interview or a presentation. It is normal to feel worried when you receive a bad medical report. Worry is a human emotion. Worry is normal. Something about that truth makes me feel relieved. Everyone feels worried from time to time. I want that truth to sink in before you read any further. Rewrite this sentence in the space below: "Worry is a normal response to a stressful situation."

_____

_____

Worry presents itself as mental distress or anguish. Worry keeps you up at night. It causes your mind to race and think about every bad thing that might happen. I think we can all agree that worry is not good for us. It disrupts our lives. It causes us to miss out on happiness and joy. In the space below, write out ways worry has affected your life:

_____

_____

_____

_____

When you and I worry, it is often about something that has not actually happened. When we experience difficulty in our lives, we are prone to think about the bad things that could happen. Our thoughts get stuck in worry. Sometimes worry comes and goes without causing too much damage to our lives, but other times worry becomes excessive or chronic.

This happens when worry becomes a persistent pattern in our lives. Excessive worrying means your thoughts are stuck in a vicious cycle of negativity. You may experience some mild physical symptoms, but mostly, excessive worry happens only inside your mind. Negative thoughts of what bad thing is happening or might happen in the future steal your joy and make you less engaged with the world around you. When worry hangs around and becomes excessive, it can cause you to live with an underlying fear, like a dark cloud following you wherever you go. Excessive worry puts you in a danger zone physically and mentally. Now that we understand more about worry, let's dive into defining stress.

WHAT IS STRESS?

Stress is how your body responds to something stressful. When you face something stressful, your body produces chemicals and hormones to help you during that stressful situation. Stress is not necessarily bad. Many wonderful things in our lives can feel stressful. Getting married can feel stressful but it is a beautiful life experience. Having a baby can be stressful but what joy a new baby brings into our lives. Stress is a part of life and often, stress is the driving factor that helps us get things done. Mild to moderate stress can actually be beneficial. Below are some positive effects of stress:

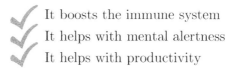
It boosts the immune system
It helps with mental alertness
It helps with productivity

God designed our bodies to handle stress. Let me repeat this important fact. God designed our bodies to handle stress. A healthy amount of stress is good for us. It helps us be mentally sharp, emotionally strong, and overall healthier.

Stress is like most things. A little bit is manageable but too much of it can turn into something harmful. Too much stress can cause harm to our minds and bodies. When you face highly stressful situations frequently, you may develop chronic stress. If not handled correctly, chronic stress can affect you in a negative way.

Common situations that cause chronic stress include financial problems, problems at work, problems in our family, divorce, experiencing the loss of someone you love, and the list goes on. Life is stressful, but God knew it would be. When God created our bodies, He gave us an alert system that is activated through our nervous system to warn us of danger. This alert system is called the "fight or flight" response. When we are in a stressful situation, our bodies produce hormones and chemicals that signal for us to either fight back or flee the situation.

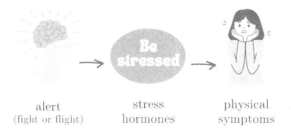

alert
(fight or flight)

stress
hormones

physical
symptoms

Two examples of stress hormones are cortisol and adrenaline. Cortisol helps control your body's metabolism and adrenaline signals the blood vessels to send blood toward your heart and lungs. Examples of stress chemicals are inflammatory proteins that affect the immune system. God designed our bodies to produce these hormones and chemicals during times of stress to help protect us from danger. When our alert system (fight or flight) is activated, and stress hormones and chemicals are released into our bodies, we experience physical symptoms that are not pleasant.

PHYSICAL SYMPTOMS OF STRESS

- ☐ Increased heart rate
- ☐ Increased blood pressure
- ☐ Increased breathing rate
- ☐ Hyper-alertness
- ☐ Stomach pain and cramping
- ☐ Headaches
- ☐ Confusion
- ☐ Memory loss
- ☐ Appetite changes
- ☐ Irritability
- ☐ Insomnia

Check the boxes above of any physical symptoms you have experienced recently due to stress. In the space below, make a list of which symptoms you experience most when your life is stressful.

_____

_____

_____

_____

_____

_____

_____

Understanding what causes you to feel stressed is an important piece of overcoming excessive worry. Make a list below of situations that cause you to feel stressed:

_____

_____

_____

_____

_____

_____

_____

_____

_____

When you feel stressed, what do you typically do to manage the stress you feel?

_____

_____

_____

_____

_____

_____

 When God designed our bodies, He thought of everything! Not only did He give us an alert system, He also gave us a calming mechanism to help us feel more peaceful. These calming hormones and chemicals help us relax.

19

Throughout the day, your nervous system (which includes the brain, spinal cord, and a network of nerves that go throughout your body), sends messages back and forth between your brain and your body. God designed this complex system to help regulate stress. Your body is designed to balance stress and calmness through hormones and chemicals.

Let me give you an example.

If you are in a lot of traffic, and someone runs a red light and almost hits your car, how do you respond? You may honk your horn and say something ugly, but what does your body do? Your God-given alert system kicks in. Adrenaline, cortisol, and other stress hormones and chemicals are released which make you feel shaky. Your heart rate goes up, you start to breathe faster and you feel hyper-alert. This is a stressful situation, so your body responds exactly the way God designed it to respond. But, the story does not end there. Those stressful feelings you just experienced do not last forever. Within a few minutes, when you realize everything is okay, your body begins to feel calm again.

Your heart rate goes back to normal. Your breathing slows down. You begin to feel more relaxed. This happens because your body releases calming hormones and chemicals like GABA and serotonin. These hormones and chemicals fight back against the stressful responses inside your body.

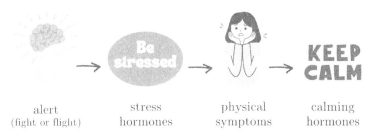

| alert | stress | physical | calming |
| (fight or flight) | hormones | symptoms | hormones |

Isn't God's design amazing? He gives us exactly what we need, right when we need it! Now that we have examined what worry and stress are, let's move on to anxiety.

WHAT IS ANXIETY?

When excessive worry and stress come together, anxiety is the result. Anxiety involves both the mind and the body. It is an overall general feeling of nervousness that can also cause emotional distress. It is normal to feel anxious from time to time, especially when you are going through a highly stressful experience, but anxiety can become chronic and lead to a bigger medical concern.

Chronic anxiety happens for a variety of reasons. A few factors that may contribute to chronic anxiety are:
- a traumatic event
- family history of chronic anxiety
- living or working in a highly stressful environment

When someone experiences chronic anxiety, their fight or flight response system may be stuck in overdrive. The stressful hormones and chemicals overpower the calming ones. When this happens, increased symptoms of stress occur. For example, headaches may develop into migraines. Stomach cramping may develop into a more serious gastrointestinal concern like irritable bowel syndrome. An overly engaged nervous system can cause physical symptoms that can be difficult to manage. If you feel you are suffering from this type of anxiety, I encourage you to talk with your primary healthcare provider about how you feel. Although this book is intended to be a tool for overcoming excessive worry, this book is not a substitute for a professional medical diagnosis or treatment. Life is hard and sometimes we experience traumatic events which cause our bodies to have anxiety that overtakes our lives.

There is a spectrum of anxiety conditions people can experience. If you are concerned about the amount of anxiety you experience, you do not have to face the way you feel, alone. Talk with your healthcare provider about the questions you have regarding any medical condition.

When might it be time to see a healthcare provider about your excessive worry or anxiety?

- If you are experiencing chronic symptoms of stress or anxiety (upset stomach, insomnia, persistent headaches, sweating for no reason, increased heart rate outside of exercise, trouble breathing).
- If you are experiencing memory loss or trouble concentrating on normal daily tasks.
- If you are worrying so much you cannot focus on your work or family life.
- If your mind races at such a fast pace, you lose track of what you are doing or where you are going.
- If you consistently feel physically agitated and cannot rest or be still.
- If you no longer enjoy things you have always enjoyed.
- If you avoid going places because you are afraid you will feel anxious.
- If you feel anxious more than you feel calm and peaceful.
- If you experience symptoms of panic (intense fear, rapid heart rate, shortness of breath, sweating, or shakiness).

Understanding the differences between worry, stress, and anxiety better equips us to overcome their effects on our lives. It also helps us understand when we may need to seek out additional support from our healthcare provider or a counselor. Here are the key definitions to keep in mind as you continue this journey to overcoming worry:

Stress: the physical response to things that are stressful
Worry: the mind dwelling on negative thoughts
Excessive worry: uncontrolled or persistent worry
Anxiety: experiencing stress and worry at the same time

Do you struggle more with stress, worry, excessive worry, or anxiety? Explain below:

_____

_____

_____

_____

_____

_____

_____

_____

_____

_____

_____

THE WHAT IF DISEASE

Sometimes worry happens because we are facing a trial in our lives and we feel out of control in that situation. Other times worry happens because we are afraid something bad *might* happen. I call this the "what if" disease. The "what if" disease is a thought pattern that happens when we are afraid of what the future may hold.

I wonder if you worry about things you are afraid might happen. Can you relate to any of these examples?

My child did not call me.
What if there has been a horrible accident?

I have a bad headache.
What if I have a brain tumor?

I did not feel good about my evaluation.
What if I lose my job?

We had an extra expense this month.
What if we can't pay the bills?

Have you ever struggled with the "what if" disease? If so, describe your situation in the space below:

_____

_____

_____

_____

_____

The "what if" disease can cause a big disruption in our lives. When thoughts about what might happen spin out of control, our thoughts run wild and can lead us to very dark places, mentally. We may focus so much on what might happen that we miss out on living in the present moment.

The "what if" disease can make us feel like there is no hope, but that is not what God says. God tells us in His Word that He is our Hope. He is our Healer. He is our Helper. In His Word, God provides the help we need to overcome worry. He does not want us to worry about what bad things might happen. He wants us to remember that no matter what happens in our lives, He has plans to give us hope and a future!

"For I know the plans I have for you," declares the Lord,
"plans to prosper you and not to harm you, plans to
give you hope and a future."
~Jeremiah 29:11

You may be saying to yourself, "That's all well and good, Joy...but how? How can I be free from the chains of excessive worry? How do I stop thinking about the bad things that might happen?" I'm so glad you asked!

The first step in overcoming excessive worry is to begin working through your worry. What do I mean by "work" through your worry? Merriam-Webster defines work as "to exert oneself physically or mentally, especially in sustained effort for a purpose or under compulsion or necessity." If we want to overcome the effects of worry in our lives, we must be ready to work through our thoughts and feelings. Work requires action. Work requires effort. Work requires determination.

Working through your worry means:
- you face your worry head-on
- you choose to be brave
- you walk by faith
- you develop new, positive habits in your life

In my journey with excessive worry, I learned I could not simply wish away my feelings. I could not jump over them, crawl under them, or run around them. I had to put in the necessary effort to walk through how I was feeling. I had to face my feelings so I could see more clearly how to manage them. Work is hard. Work is active. Work takes time, effort, energy, and participation.

"The only way out, is through."

~Robert Frost

In what way has worry stolen your joy in life?

_____

_____

_____

_____

_____

_____

_____

_____

_____

_____

How would your life be better if you could learn how to manage your worry?

_____

_____

_____

_____

_____

_____

In the remaining pages of this section, I will give you tools I want you to begin using to work through your worry. These tools are universally accepted by the medical community and have been studied in the medical literature. They have also been extremely beneficial in my personal struggle with worry.

ENCOURAGING YOUR NERVOUS SYSTEM

Earlier in this section, we took a closer look at our central nervous system and learned God gave our bodies the ability to respond to stress by releasing stress hormones and chemicals. We also learned He gave us calming hormones and chemicals. Our nervous system plays a huge role in helping us bounce back from excessive stress. Sometimes, due to chronic stress, our nervous system becomes overstimulated and we are unable to bounce back like we once could.

The encouraging news is there are things you and I can do to help our bodies release calming and feel-good hormones and chemicals. We do this by practicing certain lifestyle changes that stimulate calmness. When our nervous systems feel stuck in a state of stress, they may need a little help to fully do their job. Providing additional support to your nervous system is an important piece of working through your worry. Let's walk through several ways you can encourage your nervous system to release calming and feel-good hormones and chemicals:

LAUGHING

Do you laugh every day? Are there days when you feel too stressed and uptight to laugh? Laughing is good for you and it is one way you can fight back against stress and worry. Below are ways laughing benefits your mind and body.

- It improves the oxygen in your body which stimulates your heart and lungs.
- It increases the release of feel-good hormones and chemicals and this combats your stress levels.
- It provides a boost to your immune system.
- It helps you fight off illnesses.
- It improves pain.
- It elevates your mood.
- It improves circulation in your body which relieves tension.

So, go ahead and laugh! Did you know even a fake laugh encourages your nervous system to release calming hormones and chemicals? To help you laugh as you are reading this book, I have provided a couple of "dad jokes" below:

Why do fathers take an extra pair of socks when they go golfing?
In case they get a hole-in-one!

What did the zero say to the eight?
Wow - that belt looks good on you!

GENEROSITY

Giving generously to others, whether it is with our time or with our resources, provides a sense of purpose to our lives. The medical literature shows that generosity reduces blood pressure just as much as medicine and exercise. It also helps with chronic pain and reduces anxiety and depression. Being a generous person encourages the nervous system to produce more calming hormones and chemicals, fighting back against stress and worry.

You may already be a generous person, but if you could improve in this area, pray about ways you can give more generously to others. Not only will it bless someone...it will also be good for your nervous system!

PRAYER

Prayer is one way we connect with God. It is a lifeline in times of trouble. How often do you pray? Do you find it easy to pray or is it difficult for you to know what to say to God? Did you know that the medical literature shows that prayer and meditation play an important role in mental well-being? Prayer and meditation have been shown to decrease feelings of stress and anxiety. Prayer not only improves mental health, but it also improves the physical health of many patients.

Prayer inhibits the release of stress hormones like cortisol and adrenaline. It decreases the negative effects of stress on the body which in turn, promotes healing. Personally, prayer is essential for me to live free from the chains of worry. Talking to God and being still before Him played a crucial role in how I overcame the effects of worry on my life. Prayer sounds simple, and it can be...but sometimes when you're in a dark space of worry, it can be hard to know how to start praying.

If you do not pray as much as you would like to, I want to encourage you to make prayer an intentional, daily part of your life. You can pray anytime, anywhere. If you struggle with knowing how to pray, I have found an overall pattern of prayer that helps me in my personal prayer life. Modeled after the Lord's Prayer that Jesus taught us to pray, I find this acronym "P.R.A.Y." to be a helpful guide that enriches my prayer life.

P: Praise - begin by praising God for who He is and how He has been faithful in your life. This helps position your heart rightly before God. When we praise Him first, we open our hearts to Him with adoration and worship.

R: Repent - unconfessed sin does not affect our salvation, but it can inhibit our fellowship with God. As we seek to have a right relationship with God, it is good for us to come to God with brokenness over our sin. Repenting means we turn away from sin. Talking to God about our sin humbles us before Him.

A: Ask - asking God for what we need is a big part of prayer. He already knows all of our needs, but He wants us to come to Him and present our request to Him in faith and with confidence in Him. Ask with honesty. Ask with reverence. Ask with boldness and a humble heart.

Y: Yield to God's will - God does not grant us every prayer we ask for. He knows what's best, and as we go to Him in prayer, asking for Him to do something, we need to submit to His will. His plan is always the best plan and His timing is always perfect.

Prayer is an essential part of our lives as Christians. We need time alone with God. We need to pour our hearts out to Him and walk closely with Him. Prayer is one way we connect with God in a personal way. Think about your prayer life. How can you enrich your time with God? What new habits can you put in place to spend more time with God in prayer?

_____

_____

_____

_____

_____

_____

_____

Practice using the "P.R.A.Y." tool in your prayer life. Begin by writing out the tool below:

P

R

A

Y

DEEP BREATHING

Another strategy that helps support the work of your nervous system is to control your breathing. Paying attention to your breathing is important in managing stress. You may be surprised at how shallow your breathing is when you feel worried and anxious. Shallow breathing means your lungs are not getting a full dose of oxygen. Try letting out a big "sigh" when you feel stressed and see if you feel a little calmer.

When you experience a high amount of stress, you may find great benefits from practicing deep breathing exercises. This promotes relaxation and may calm your anxiety. These exercises modify your body's response to stress and they support your nervous system. Making deep breathing a part of your daily habits can help reduce your symptoms of worry and anxiety. For me personally, I find this technique most helpful when I use it while praying. As I pray silently to God in my mind, breathing deeply enables me to calm my mind and body. Practicing these techniques helps increase the release of calming hormones and chemicals:

- Find a quiet, comfortable space to sit or lie down.
- Close your eyes.
- Breathe normally and then take a deep breath (breathe in through your nose).
- Let your chest and belly rise up as you breathe in.
- Take it slow and let your stomach area fully rise.
- Breathe out through your mouth, slowly.
- Repeat this for 5-10 minutes.

JOURNALING

At one of the lowest points in my life, when I was trapped in a cycle of worry, God led me to a Christian counselor who encouraged me to start journaling.

Journaling sounds so simple, but this counselor explained how journaling would help me get my jumbled-up, worrisome thoughts out of my head and down on paper so I could see them. Making a grocery list of my worried thoughts helped me see what I was thinking about. When I could see them on paper, I could begin sorting through them. I could separate out what thoughts were valid and what thoughts were irrational.

The process of journaling decreased my stress and worry and helped me cope with things that were happening in my life. When I began journaling, I also found that it drew me closer to God. It grew my faith!

The best way to journal is to find a quiet place to be alone and then start writing down your thoughts and feelings. Carving out time in my day to be alone with God to journal helped me settle my heart more on Him. I was amazed at how freeing and transformational journaling was for me, and do you know what? It can be freeing and transformational for you, too! By writing down your thoughts and feelings, you face what you're worried about. You begin to understand your thoughts and feelings more clearly.

In the medical literature, there are countless articles highlighting the benefits of journaling. Journaling just a few days each week can lead to improved well-being and decreased mental distress. Journaling not only benefits your mental health but it can improve your overall health. The act of writing down your thoughts and feelings is a healthy habit you can incorporate into your life to help manage your anxiety. It is an important tool you can use to decrease stress and worry.

You may be wondering how to begin journaling or how long should it take. It is important to understand there is no one-size-fits-all method for journaling. Some people prefer to have a nice, pretty journal to write in so they can save their journal entries. Other people write out their thoughts and feelings on plain paper and then rip up the paper. This is referred to as the "write it out and rip it up method." Some people journal for five minutes a day, while other people journal for over an hour.

Journaling is personal and is meant to be private. Your thoughts belong to you, and journaling should be a safe place you can express how you really feel. You should journal in a way that makes the most sense for you. What is most important is that you get alone with God and start writing.

As you begin the process of working through your worry, I hope you feel encouraged to face your struggle with worry head-on! You can be free from the damaging effects of worry, but it will require hard work and practice. The starting point is an open and honest heart that is ready for action!

Journaling is one of the best places to begin. I hope your heart is open and your pen is ready. Grab some paper or a journal and find a quiet place to be alone with God. I have provided a journaling guide on the next page that you can use to get started. I am excited for you to take this first step as you begin working through your worry.

JOURNALING GUIDE

As you begin to work through your worry through journaling, consider the tips below to help you begin:

- Get alone with God (set aside intentional time with Him).

- Pray and ask Him for His help.

- Be completely honest. Hold nothing back.

- Look up scripture that encourages your heart.

- Ask God to speak to you through His Word.

- Write down whatever comes to your mind.

- Take as little or as much time as you need.

Consider answering these questions as you start writing:

- What are the most difficult experiences you have faced in your life? How did you overcome them?

- When is the first time you remember struggling with excessive worry?

- What does your worry look and feel like?

- What are you worried about right now?

- How does worry and anxiety affect your life?

- Do you believe you can trust God with your life?

- Do you believe God can help you with your worry? Why or why not?

A Prescription for Joy

STEP ONE

Name _____

Date _____

_____

_____

Memorize the p.r.a.y. tool

Set aside time each day to pray

Practice deep breathing exercises as needed

Laugh at least three times every day

Give generously to others

Use the journaling guide to begin journaling

_____   Dr. Joy

Date   Signature

A prayer for working through your worry

God, thank You for loving me. Thank You for reminding me that there is nothing and no one as powerful as You. I believe You can take my struggle with worry and use it for something good. You can turn it around. I believe You have a hope and a future for my life. I want to be free from the effects of worrying too much. I want to be free of the effects of living in fear. Please help me face my feelings head-on. Please help me be brave as I work through my worry. I put my trust in You. Amen.

And we know that in all things God works for the good of those who love him, who have been called according to his purpose.
~Romans 8:28

Thoughts from Step One

Take a few minutes to write down what encouraged you from this section. What main points do you want to remember and use in your life?

_____

_____

_____

_____

_____

_____

_____

_____

_____

_____

_____

_____

_____

_____

_____

_____

_____

_____

_____

_____

Step Two

OVERCOME FEAR

FEAR HAS NO CONTROL OVER YOU

Step Two: Overcome Fear

How would you finish this sentence? My greatest fear is...

_____

_____

_____

_____

   For much of my life, my greatest fear was a tornado would hit my house with me inside. With a fear like that, you would think I lived in a state where tornadoes happen frequently, but that is not true. I have lived most of my life in the heart of North Carolina where we do not experience many tornadoes. So, why was I so afraid of tornadoes? I blame it on Dorothy.

   I remember being terrified watching The Wizard of Oz as a little girl. If you have seen the movie, you know the "twister" scene. Dorothy and her little dog, Toto, are coming home only to find a massive tornado is heading toward them. Dorothy cannot find her family. She tries to open the storm cellar, but the winds are too strong. Debris is flying everywhere so Dorothy goes into the farmhouse and is knocked unconscious by an old window, plunging her into a dreamy sleep. Dorothy, Toto, and the house are swept away by the tornado.

   As I watched the movie, I was so afraid that I ran and hid behind my Daddy's avocado green chair. I just knew Dorothy and Toto were doomed. I guess that fear stuck with me because as long as I can remember, I have been terrified of tornadoes. Throughout my life I had dreams of tornadoes coming toward my house with me inside. I would wake up right before the tornado hit and I would be so relieved it was only a dream. Little did I know one day I would come face-to-face with my greatest fear.

In 1916, my great-grandfather built a farmhouse for his family on their farm in North Carolina. From the front porch, you could see for miles.

Throughout the years, the old farmhouse was remodeled and used for different family members to live in. Shortly after Bryan and I were married, we decided to build our house on the family farm. In the summer of 1999, we lived in the farmhouse while our new home was under construction.

On September 29, 1999, I was working as a pharmacist in a clinic about 20 miles from home. I remember how strange the sky looked on the drive home. There was an unusual hue to the sky and an odd feeling in the air. Bryan had a meeting at church that evening, so after supper he left for his meeting, and I started cleaning the kitchen. Shortly after he left, my father-in-law, Bill, called our house to warn us about the weather.

It is hard to comprehend, but back in 1999, we did not have

sophisticated cell phones like we do today. There was no enhanced weather alert system that popped up on our phones. Unless you were lucky enough to have a weather radio in your house, you had to watch the news or the weather channel to know when severe weather was in the area. Of course there are always people in our lives who are weather enthusiasts and I would put my father-in-law in that category.

As long as I have known my father-in-law, Bill, he has had a weather radio. It was not unusual for him to call us to warn us about an approaching storm, but on this particular day, his phone call was different. It was more serious. There was a sense of concern and urgency in his voice as he told me a tornado was in the area and for me to take cover!

You can imagine how shocked I was. Could it be that a tornado was headed my way? I am in the middle of washing spaghetti noodles off of the dishes and now my life is in danger? I ran out onto the large, screened-in porch on the back of the house and looked across the field. The sky still looked unusual, and the wind was blowing, but there was no sign of a tornado. I thought surely Bill was overreacting. I hung up the phone with him and quickly called my Daddy. My Daddy is a farmer and if there's anyone who knows about the weather, it is my Daddy. He wants to know about the weather! He was watching the news and said the radar was clear.

It was at that very moment, while I was still standing on the back screened-in porch talking to my Daddy that the wind picked up and I saw a tornado taking shape in the sky. My heart sank. It felt surreal. I shouted with panic in my voice, "I see it - I see it! It's coming straight for me!" And then...the phone went dead. I froze. I had a flashback to my days in elementary school when we practiced tornado drills.

Back then, I remember learning that a brick house was the safest type of house to be in, and a basement was the best place to go if a tornado was in the area. I had no brick house and no basement. What in the world was I going to do? Even though I felt panicked, I knew I needed to protect my little dog. In case you are wondering; no...my little dog's name was not Toto, it was Sadie. She was in her dog pen next to the big oak tree.

With a panicked feeling in my chest, I ran out the screened door as fast as I could to get her from her dog pen. The wind began to blow harder as we ran inside. I quickly slammed the door and went to the center of the farmhouse foyer. I knelt down on the hardwood floor. Holding Sadie tightly in my arms, I could hear the wind howling like I had never heard before. I quietly prayed, "God, please protect me."

The tornado was barreling across the field as Sadie and I huddled together in the foyer. I was shaking with fear, and I held her tightly against my chest as the roaring sound grew louder and louder. I hunched over and put my face next to hers as I cried out to God, "Please protect me!" It felt like time stood still as I braced for the impact. My mind was racing, and my heart was overwhelmed with fear. The noise was so loud, I could barely think. I knew Sadie and I were in serious danger. Then...it hit.

The roaring sound, the shaking of the house, the rattling of the glass windows, the sound of outside debris being ripped to shreds, and the fear of dying. I was petrified. Sadie whimpered and I continued to pray. I heard a very loud crash and the deafening roar of the tornado quickly turned into deafening silence. Within a few seconds, it was over, and Sadie and I were still alive! Once I realized I had not died, my "fight or flight" response kicked in. I wanted to GET OUT OF THAT

HOUSE as fast as I could! I was physically shaking as I ran to open the kitchen door that led to the screened-in porch. I held Sadie tightly in my arms as I frantically tried to leave the house. When I pulled on the doorknob, the door would not open. The wall of the kitchen was leaning inward causing the door to jam. My heart was racing like I was running an Olympic sprint as I jerked the doorknob as hard as I could several times. I was breathing fast as I pulled the door with all my might and finally, it opened just enough for Sadie and me to squeeze through.

Do you remember what happened in The Wizard of Oz when Dorothy's farmhouse landed in Munchkinland? She opened her farmhouse door to find a magical land full of vibrant colors and a yellow brick road. That is not what happened when I opened my farmhouse door. When I stepped onto the screened-in porch, a huge oak tree was laying on top of the house.

Remember the crash I heard when the tornado hit? That noise was a 70-year-old oak tree falling on top of the farmhouse. The old tree had a giant root system that had anchored it down in the ground for decades. The tornado ripped the tree up from its roots and tossed it on top of the farmhouse. Tree branches, leaves, and debris were everywhere. I was so afraid the tree was going to fall through the screened-in porch. Sadie and I quickly made our way off of the screened-in porch and I could clearly see all of the damage. I could not believe the devastation. Outbuildings that had been on the farm for 100 years were ripped apart. Pieces of metal roofing were twisted into coil shapes from the impact of the tornado. Glass covered the driveway from the broken windows of my great-grandmother's flower house. Sadie's flattened dog pen was lying against the house. If I would not have taken her with me into the house, she would have surely died. The portable potty that was at the construction site of our new house had been hurled into the air and was hanging on the power line. My car which was parked in the driveway was totaled. Bryan's aluminum fishing boat was destroyed. I looked at all the damage in disbelief and I was overtaken with fear and confusion. I did not know what to do.

Fear can paralyze you from knowing what to do next. Have you ever experienced something in your life that caused paralyzing fear? Explain below:

_____

_____

_____

_____

_____

_____

_____

_____

_____

_____

_____

_____

_____

_____

_____

Fear. It is not a warm and fuzzy word. Most of us do not like to feel afraid, yet we all feel afraid of certain things. Some of the most common things people are afraid of include public speaking, having a terminal illness, going to the dentist, spiders and snakes.

Fear is not a "feel good" word, but not all fear is bad. In certain situations, fear is actually a good thing. Having a healthy type of fear prevents us from making unwise choices, like jumping off of a ten-story building or driving 95 miles an hour down the highway. This type of fear helps us make good decisions about things that may cause us harm.

Another healthy type of fear we can have is how we respond to God. God tells us in His Word we should fear Him. Let's take a look at a few verses:

The fear of the LORD leads to life,
So that one may sleep satisfied, untouched by evil.
~Proverbs 19:23

But be sure to fear the Lord and serve him faithfully
with all your heart; consider what great things
he has done for you.
~1 Samuel 12:24

Serve the Lord with fear and rejoice with trembling.
~Psalm 2:11

Fearing the Lord refers to positioning ourselves *rightly* before God in humble reverence to Him. Fearing Him means we are in awe of His holiness. It means we revere and honor Him. He is the one true God, worthy of our worship. He is not only our Savior, He is also our Lord.

Fearing God gives us wisdom, and fearing Him is an important part of pleasing Him.

His pleasure is not in the strength of the horse, nor his delight in the legs of the warrior; the Lord delights in those who fear him, who put their hope in his unfailing love.
~Psalm 147:10-11

We see from God's Word that some fear is positive, but there is also an unhealthy type of fear. This type of fear is described in the book of 2 Timothy as having a "spirit of fear," and it is not from God.

For God has not given us a spirit of fear, but of power and of love and of a sound mind.
~2 Timothy 1:7

God gives us a spirit of power, love, and a sound mind, but Satan works against God. His mission is to destroy us. He is the one who brings us a spirit of fear. A spirit of fear is a cowardly fear that leads us away from trusting God. When we are consumed with this cowardly fear, we live our lives bound to and limited by what we are afraid of. It can overtake us and prevent us from living the life God intends for us to live. Worry is rooted in this kind of fear. The second step in overcoming excessive worry is to overcome fear. When we struggle with excessive worry, we can usually trace it back to fear. Satan uses fear to rob us of joy, fulfillment, and contentment in life.

For example, we can be so fearful of financial ruin that we worry about money, hoarding every penny we earn. We can be so fearful of getting hurt emotionally, that we worry about the risks of growing close to another person, limiting our relationships with others.

Fear also plays a major role in the "what if" disease. Fear dominates our thoughts about what might happen. Consider this example:

Fear: I am afraid of getting cancer

Problem: I have a bad headache

What if: What if I have a brain tumor

Worry: If I have cancer, then I will have to go through cancer treatments which will cost a lot of money and burden my family. I will be out of work and that will ruin us financially. I will be sick and unable to take care of my family. I might die. My children will grow up without their mother and be scarred for life...

Sound familiar?

Worry is rooted in this kind of fear, but there is good news, my friend. When you uncover and rip up the roots of fear, you begin to overcome your worry. But how? How can you uncover your fears? By being brave and turning on the light. When I was little, like many children, I was afraid there was a monster living under my bed. It seems silly now but in the mind of a seven-year-old girl fearing a monster is a serious thing. Night after night, I would lay in the middle of my bed worried this monster would get me. I was so afraid, I would not even stretch out my arm to hang over the side of my bed. Maybe you felt that way too when you were a child. One night I needed to go to the bathroom so badly, but I was too afraid to get out of bed. I had a decision to make. I could either wet my bed or I could get up and go to the bathroom, risking being eaten by this monster under my bed.

I don't know why, but that night, I found my courage. I was going to find out if there was a monster under my bed. I reached over to turn on the lamp beside my bed. I eased my way out of bed, got down on the floor, and pulled back the bed skirt. Do you know what I found? I saw clothes, shoes, and old papers, but there was no monster. From that night on, I was never again afraid of a monster living under my bed. By facing my fear, I realized I had nothing to fear. I was confident there was no monster under my bed. I had no reason to worry. I uncovered the truth by turning on the light.

Worry is a strange thing. It often comes without warning. It cannot always be explained. It dominates your thoughts and even though you know your thoughts are irrational, you still worry. That is what happened to me with the tornado.

Over the next few weeks, after the tornado hit the farmhouse, the storm damage was cleaned up, the big oak tree was removed from the farmhouse, the inside of the farmhouse was repaired, and life got back to normal. Well, almost. I was not the same.

In the months to come, I found myself in a very dark place emotionally. A spirit of fear came over my life that plunged me into a struggle with worry like I had never experienced before. I had trouble sleeping and eating. My mind could not stay focused on the things I needed to do. My relationships suffered. I had feelings of gloom and doom come over me for no apparent reason and I had a feeling of nervousness that did not make sense.

You would think I would be so happy that I survived this tornado, but instead, this experience sent me spinning into a cycle of worry. During this time in my life, I prayed a lot. I read my Bible a lot. I also cried a lot. I had not lost my faith in God. I knew He loved me. I did not doubt God's faithfulness. I knew He was with me, yet I could not stop myself from worrying. I could not stop my mind from dwelling on the bad things that had happened and the bad things that might happen. It felt overwhelming to me.

I felt like that seven-year-old little girl again, lying in the middle of my bed, afraid of a monster that I could not see. I needed the courage to turn on the light so I could see the monster that was living in my head. But how?

The Lord is my light and my salvation—whom shall I fear?
The Lord is the stronghold of my life—
of whom shall I be afraid?
~Psalm 27:1

Being courageous to turn on the light to my fear meant I needed to face my fears head-on. That's what I want you to do, too. As you continue to work through your worry, I want you to find the courage to face your fears. One way to do this is by writing down what you are afraid of. Searching your heart over what is causing you to feel afraid is an important piece of overcoming worry. As you write out your thoughts and feelings, you are turning on the light in the darkness of your heart and mind. You uncover your fears as you write out how you feel. I will provide you with journaling questions at the end of this section to begin writing down your fears. By writing them down, you are turning on the light to the fears living inside your heart and mind. What a beautiful truth to know that the light will always overcome the darkness.

The light shines in the darkness, and the darkness can never extinguish it.
~John 1:5

In addition to uncovering your fears through journaling, I want to encourage you to make the life-changing decision to trust in God even when you feel afraid. It's easy to trust in God when life is good. It is much harder to trust in Him when we are fearful.

Trust in the Lord with all your heart and lean not on your own understanding; in all your ways submit to him, and he will make your paths straight.
~Proverbs 3:5-6

Trust is one of the foundations of a healthy relationship. Without trust, it is nearly impossible to have a happy, healthy relationship. In order for us to walk closely with God, we need to put our trust in Him. Trusting in God when life is hard means you choose to allow your faith to be bigger than your fear. It means you no longer give fear a dominating voice in your life. It means you choose to stand on truth. Faith in Jesus is truth. Fear from Satan is a lie. Take a minute and say that out loud, "Faith in Jesus is truth. Fear from Satan is a lie."

Instead of allowing fear to overtake your heart and mind, choose to be confident in who God is. Trust is not wishful thinking. Biblical trust is defined as confident, sure, and bold. This means we are sure of Him. We know who He is. We know His character.

- He is love.
- He is good.
- He is holy.
- He is righteous.
- He is forgiving.
- He is accepting.
- He is all-powerful.
- He is all-knowing.
- He is Healer, Helper, and our heavenly Father.

God is loving, kind, and good, but the age-old question remains - why does He allow bad things to happen? It's a tough question to answer, but I've come to realize the danger in trying to explain a holy God with a human mind. God's ways are not my ways. His thoughts are not my thoughts. My ways and thoughts are flawed. His ways and thoughts are perfect.

"For my thoughts are not your thoughts, neither are your ways my ways," declares the Lord. "As the heavens are higher than the earth, so are my ways higher than your ways and my thoughts than your thoughts."
~Isaiah 55:8-9

Everything God allows to happen in our lives is because He is working together His good plan, but that does not mean everything that happens to us will be good. There is nothing good about terminal diseases. There is nothing good about sexual abuse. There is nothing good about adultery. There is nothing good about horrific accidents. There is nothing good about tornadoes. But, there is something very good about God, and He has the power to take the most terrible situation and use it for something good. In the painful times of life, we can find comfort in knowing that behind the scenes, a trustworthy God sits on His throne. When we belong to Him, we can be *sure* He is working all things together (even the bad things) for something good.

As followers of Christ, when we make the life-changing decision to trust in God, we choose to walk by faith, not by how we feel. This is when our faith overrides our fear. Choosing to trust in God means we may not feel like it, but we make the choice to trust in Him. This decision leads us to joy, even in the middle of feeling afraid.

When you face a situation that causes you to be afraid, remember...it's not your job to try to figure out what God is doing or why He is doing it. It's your job to love Him, trust in Him, and surrender to Him. Real faith is when you trust in Him even when you don't understand what He is doing. When something bad happens, you can be sure God is allowing it because it will bring about something good. He loves you and no matter what you go through in this life...He promises to be with you.

Just as God is good and He loves and cares for you, Satan is the father of lies and he will use fear to place you in a state of bondage. He wants you to doubt God and he wants fear to drive you to be an ineffective Christian. Satan will use fear to deceive you!

You are of your father the devil, and your will is to do your father's desires. He was a murderer from the beginning, and has nothing to do with the truth, because there is no truth in him. When he lies, he speaks out of his own character, for he is a liar and the father of lies.
~John 8:44

Satan uses fear against you. He knows that fear causes worry, anxiety, loneliness, and depression. He wants you to focus on how you feel instead of what you know to be true. He wants to shake your faith. Don't listen to him, my friend. Instead, choose to respond to your fear with a heart and mind full of courage!

When I am afraid, I put my trust in you. In God, whose word I praise—in God I trust and am not afraid. What can mere mortals do to me?
~Psalm 56:3-4

Over and over again in His Word, God tells us to be brave and courageous. I think this is because God knows Satan will use fear to try to take us down. I'm encouraged when I remember that God's love is stronger than my fear. God's love is powerful. His love for us overcomes any fear Satan tries to throw our way.

The next time a wave of fear rises up in you, change your focus away from the fear you are feeling and instead, focus on how much you are loved by God. You can be strong and courageous because you serve a fierce and mighty God!

Don't be afraid, for I am with you.
-Isaiah 41:10a

Say these statements out loud:

- Fear has no power over my mind.
- Fear has no power over my heart.
- Fear has no power over my life.
- God is for me and His power is with me!

In the midst of our uncertainty, we can choose to trust in God. We can put our trust in Him when life is going our way, and we can put our trust in Him when life is falling apart. When Satan says, "Be afraid," God says, "Trust in Me!"

When I am afraid, I put my trust in you.
~Psalm 56:3

TURN ON THE LIGHT TO THE FEAR IN YOUR LIFE

Answer these questions about
fear in your journal:

- What is your earliest memory of feeling afraid?

- How do you normally respond to feeling afraid?

- What does "face your fears head-on" mean to you?

- Make a list of all your fears (don't hold back). Divide up the list into two columns:
    - One column of fears that are likely to happen
    - Another column of fears that are unlikely to happen

- Why do you think you have this list of fears?

- What do you need to do today to overcome your fears?

- What has this section helped you learn about fear?

- Can you trust in God even when you are afraid? Explain.

A Prescription for Joy
STEP TWO

R̶X̶ Name _____

Date _____

_____

Journal about your fears

Memorize 2 Timothy 1:7

Memorize Psalm 56:3

Make a list of God's promises

Put your complete trust in God

Dr. Joy

_____

Date   Signature

A prayer for overcoming fear

Lord, sometimes my struggle with worry makes me feel like I am in a dark place. It can be hard to find my way out. Will You please help me remember that You are the light of the world? You want my faith in You to overcome the fear that I feel. Worry is rooted in fear. Will You help me rip up the roots of fear that live within my heart and mind? As I seek to overcome fear in my life, remind me that I can trust in You. When life is good, I can trust in You. When life is hard, I can trust in You. I need You, Lord. I love You. Amen.

When Jesus spoke again to the people, he said, "I am the light of the world. Whoever follows me will never walk in darkness, but will have the light of life."
~John 8:12

Thoughts from Step Two

Take a few minutes to write down what encouraged you from this section. What main points do you want to remember and use in your life?

_____

_____

_____

_____

_____

_____

_____

_____

_____

_____

_____

_____

_____

_____

_____

_____

_____

_____

_____

Step Three

RECLAIM YOUR THOUGHTS

LOVING GOD WITH YOUR MIND

Step Three: Reclaim Your Thoughts

Most of my childhood took place in the '80s. I loved parachute pants, leg warmers, and tight-rolled jeans. Oh, and we cannot forget our BIG hairstyles. I wish I knew how many cans of Aqua Net hair spray my sister and I used. Each morning before school, after we put in our shoulder pads, we made our hair as big as possible...and that required lots of hairspray! I feel sure we contributed to the depletion of the ozone layer because we left a cloud of hairspray in the air every time we left our bathroom.

One of the biggest movies in the '80s was Karate Kid. Goodness...I think all elementary and middle school girls had a crush on Daniel, or "Danielson" as Mr. Miyagi fondly named him. There was a very important scene in the movie that I would like us to revisit. Let me describe it for you:

Daniel was eager to learn karate because he was being bullied at school. He met Mr. Miyagi and he agreed to teach Daniel karate. Daniel came to Mr. Miyagi's house each day, proudly wearing his hachimaki (Japanese headband) for his karate lessons, but his first few lessons only involved doing chores for Mr. Miyagi. To Daniel, these chores seemed unrelated to learning karate. Mr. Miyagi gave him detailed instructions on how he was to do each of these chores. He painted the house, painted the fence, sanded the floors, and waxed the cars each with specific motions. The infamous lines "wax on, wax off" ring in my ears as I remember the movie.

Daniel worked for days, hours at a time, doing these chores until he was fed up! Frustration got the best of Daniel because he wanted to learn karate, not how to do all of these chores. He confronted Mr. Miyagi in anger telling him he was tired of doing all this work!

Mr. Miyagi said (in broken English), "Not everything is as seems," and he called Daniel over and asked him to demonstrate how he does the chores. One by one, Daniel showed Mr. Miyagi how he does each chore; paint the fence, sand the floors, and wax the cars. As he demonstrated each motion, all of a sudden, Mr. Miyagi began using karate against him. Instinctively, Daniel was able to defend himself by using the motions he learned while doing the chores.

Daniel did not realize it, but through hard work and repetition of doing each chore, he learned fundamental blocking karate moves. Because he practiced these chores every day, these moves became second nature to him. He *had* been learning karate the whole time...he just didn't know it.

I want you to keep this story in mind as you continue reading. So far in this book, we have reviewed what happens in our bodies when we feel afraid. We have looked at the importance of working through our worry through journaling and by encouraging our nervous system.

Journaling is a great habit to instill into your life as it helps you see your worried and fearful thoughts, but journaling is not helpful when worry strikes your mind when you are driving down the highway. It is not practical (or safe) to pull over on the side of the interstate and begin journaling every time you feel a wave of worry come over you.

Like Daniel, you need to be able to defend yourself when the enemy attacks you. Well, my friend, put on your hachimaki. In this section, I will provide you with strategies you can use to take back control of your thought life. I will also provide you with practical tools you can begin using today to help you overcome worry. These strategies and tools will take practice, but the more you practice them, the more they will become second nature to you.

The third step in overcoming worry is to learn how to reclaim your thoughts. To reclaim means to take back control of something. In your struggle with worry, you need to take back control of your thoughts. Your thoughts are powerful. What you think about has a lot to do with the quality and direction of your life. What you think about, matters.

OUR INNER VOICE - SELF TALK

Our minds are constantly active when we are awake. We have internal thoughts racing around in our minds when we are conscious. Most of us have an internal monologue or internal "self-talk" that goes on inside our minds. This inner voice gives life to our thoughts. Our inner voice helps us understand and engage with the world around us without speaking out loud. It is rare for someone not to experience this inner voice. It is there to help us complete everyday tasks, organize our thoughts and cancel out other distractions around us. Working on a project that requires concentration is a place our inner voice shines. You may not say out loud what you are thinking, but you hear yourself talking inside your head as you think through each step in your project.

This internal narrative can be very helpful when you solve a problem or work through a question, but sometimes your inner voice is not so nice. Let me elaborate. When you are getting ready each morning, what does your inner voice say when you look in the mirror? Maybe like me, your inner voice reminds you of your flaws. My inner voice reminds me of how I have aged or how I look tired. It often reminds me of what is wrong with my life instead of what is right with my life. Maybe you can relate? Our internal voice can be our enemy, and this is true when we struggle with worry. The messages we receive from our inner voice during seasons of worry are mostly negative. Our inner voice spews out worrisome thoughts, like these:

"I am not going to make it. I can't do this. I might die. My son may never come home. I will never feel normal again. This stress is going to kill me! My marriage is terrible. I will never be happy." Do any of those sound familiar? Reclaiming our thoughts begins with recognizing what thoughts are in our heads. We need to become more aware of our internal voice because what we think about makes a difference in our lives. Our thoughts shape who we are. They are powerful, and God has a lot to say to us in His Word about the power of our thoughts.

Set your minds on things that are above, not on things that are on earth.
~Colossians 3:2

We destroy arguments and every lofty opinion raised against the knowledge of God, and take every thought captive to obey Christ.
~2 Corinthians 10:5

Do not conform to the pattern of this world but be transformed by the renewing of your mind. Then you will be able to test and approve what God's will is - his good, pleasing, and perfect will.
~Romans 12:2

In the passage of scripture above, Paul tells believers they need to change their old way of thinking. He impresses upon their hearts that they need to be transformed. They need to be changed.

Often, we know we need to be changed, but we don't know what we need to do to find that transformation. We wonder how we can transform into who God wants us to be. Paul answers this question when he tells believers that transformation occurs through the renewing of their minds. He encourages them to do away with ungodly thoughts and replace them with thoughts that honor Jesus. You see friend, your transformation begins in your thought life. It begins in your mind. Through my personal struggle with worry and anxiety, I learned how important it was for me to examine my thoughts. By examining my personal thought life, I saw a glimpse into the direction my life was headed. Throughout the day, negative, self-damaging thoughts popped in and out of my mind. I learned not every thought that came into my mind had permission to stay there. I learned I had control over what thoughts took up residence in my mind.

Let me ask you a question. Do you like spiders?

Have you ever found a spider in your house? If so, what did you do with it? Did you make a little bed for it and feed it good food so it could live with you? Of course not. You found a large item to smack it with or you were more gracious to the spider and took it outside to live. Whether you are a spider exterminator or a spider relocator, you want the spider out of your house!

This is how I want you to think about your thought life. Consider your mind as your home. It is a place you value. It is a place you take care of and guard. Consider your negative, anxious thought as the spider. You did not invite it in, but it showed up anyway. Regardless of how that anxious thought arrived in your mind, it is important you recognize it and deal with it in order to protect your mind.

When an anxious thought pops into your mind, YOU have the power to decide what happens to that thought. A thought has no power over you. It is just a thought. It only becomes powerful when you allow it to take up residence in your mind. It only becomes powerful when you choose to dwell on it.

I hope you will embrace this truth: YOU have control over your thought life. You get to decide which thoughts are allowed to stay in your mind and which ones must leave. It may sound simple, but you *can* change the channel on your thoughts.

CHANGE THE CHANNEL

When I think back on my childhood, I have vivid memories of watching my favorite cartoons on Saturday mornings. I loved Bugs Bunny, Sylvester, Tweety Bird, and all of the Looney Toons characters, but the Flintstones were my favorite! I have such fond memories of pouring myself a large bowl of Lucky Charms and sitting on the floor of my den in my nightgown as I heard *Yabadabadoo* come across the TV. My sister and I had lap desks we used as TV trays. I would sit as close as possible to the TV to watch cartoons, and I would watch as long as my mom would allow.

It is so hard to believe back in those days, televisions only had a few channels. There was no such thing as streaming movies or shows online. There was no internet. Houses had big antennas on top of their roofs that scanned the area to pick up broadcast signals from television networks.

In the early '80s, we did not have a way to record television shows and watch them later. Our TV did not have a remote control either. I could not sit on the couch and quickly surf through channels. If I did not like what was on, I had to get up off the couch and turn the big round knob on the TV to change the channel. Back in those days, changing the channel took some effort.

The idea of "changing the channel" is a good image to keep in mind when it comes to reclaiming our thoughts. We can change the channel in our thought life, but in order to do that, we must first pay attention to what we are thinking about. Awareness is key!

An anxious thought is like that creepy spider. It sneaks into your mind and it wants to stay there. When you realize that thought is sneaking into the life of your mind, you can find ways to stop thinking about that anxious thing. You can learn to cancel out an anxious thought and replace it with something that is good and true. You can take back control of your thought life. You can reclaim your thoughts. Changing the channel in your mind leads you down the path to JOY!

The best way to change the channel in our thought life is to replace negative, anxious thoughts with ones that align with God's truth. Reclaiming our thoughts is how we take back ownership of our thought life.

As we become more aware of our anxious and damaging thoughts, the more we realize we need to replace those thoughts with things that align with God's Word. Ask yourself these questions - "Are my thoughts aligned with God's truth? Are they pleasing to Him?"

As I have worked through reclaiming my own thoughts, these verses in Philippians have been very helpful to me. They confirm that I get to choose what I think about and that God wants me to focus on good things.

> *Finally, brothers and sisters, whatever is true,*
> *whatever is noble, whatever is right,*
> *whatever is pure, whatever is lovely,*
> *whatever is admirable—*
> *if anything is excellent or praiseworthy—*
> *think about such things.*
> *~Philippians 4:8-9*

I encourage you to memorize these verses in Philippians as you continue your journey to overcoming worry. Write down reminders on sticky notes or notecards and place them in prominent areas of your home so you see them every day. My bathroom mirror, office desk, and the steering wheel in my car have all been great places for me to put little reminders from God's Word. Putting these notes in places where I see them throughout the day serves as a reminder to me of God's truth!

Think about things that honor God.

I am what you call a "repeat learner," meaning, often, I need to be reminded of things more than once. The more I repeat it, the more automatic it becomes in my life. Maybe you are a repeat learner too? If so, little notes can be great reminders. It's easy to get wrapped up in the day-to-day stresses of life. Little notes of encouragement remind me to "change the channel" in my mind and align my thoughts with what God desires me to think about.

Philippians 4:8-9 also serves as a guide to help me manage my anxious thoughts. When an anxious thought pops into my mind and I begin to dwell on it, there are a few questions that are helpful for me to ask myself:

- Is this thought true?
- Is this thought an honest thought?
- Does this thought honor God?
- Does this thought align with God's Word?
- Is this thought rooted in goodness?
- Do I think this thought is from God?

Let's revisit that short list of damaging thoughts that commonly come into our heads. Let's see how we can change the channel and create new thoughts that line up with God's Word:

Thought: I am not going to make it.
Truth: God has a good plan for my life.
New Thought: I am going to do my best to live for Him and trust Him to help me. He is my helper!

Thought: I can't do this.
Truth: God is with me.
New Thought: I am going to rely on Him for the strength I need. He is able to do all things. There is nothing too hard for Him. If He has called me to do this, then He will enable me to do it.

Thought: My son may never come home.

Truth: God hears my prayers. God loves my son. God knows my heart.

New Thought: I am going to keep praying diligently for my son because I know I can put my trust in God.

Thought: I will never feel normal again.

Truth: God sees me and He knows how I feel. I can trust Him with my whole life.

New Thought: I will keep praying. Even when my health fails, I can choose joy as I keep my eyes on Jesus.

Thought: This stress is going to kill me!

Truth: I do not face the trials of life alone. Jesus is with me.

New Truth: God created my body to handle stressful situations. As I go through this stressful time, I will keep praying and trusting in Him.

Thought: My marriage is terrible. I will never be happy.

Truth: My joy is in Christ. Marriage is not easy, but I love my husband and I am committed to him.

New Thought: I am going to choose to focus on what is right with my spouse instead of what is wrong with him. I am going to pray for Him and I am going to ask God to help me be the best wife I can be. My joy is in Christ, not in people.

For those who live according to the flesh set their minds
on the things of the flesh, but those who live according
to the Spirit set their minds on the things of the Spirit.
~Romans 8:5

Changing the channel on negative, damaging thoughts can change how worry affects you. Reminding yourself of the truth of God's Word is a great step toward fighting back against worry. When you fill your mind up with God's Word there is not enough room for worry and fear to take root.

EXAMINING OUR HABITS

Do you have any bad habits? I do, and as I struggled to overcome excessive worry, I realized that some of my bad habits were breeding grounds for worry and anxiety.

God designed the human mind with amazing abilities. Our minds are like sponges. They have the ability to absorb and internalize things around us. They soak up what they are exposed to. In fact, I would say the direction we set our minds to affects the direction of our lives. Our mindset is like a compass for our lives. It helps to navigate our lives. So, the question arises, what direction are we setting our minds to go?

The world sends messages to us wherever we go. We are inundated with billboards, television commercials, radio ads, music, social media, etc. These marketing platforms are designed to influence your attitudes and opinions or to sell you something. Did you know the background music that plays in grocery stores is specifically chosen to encourage shoppers to spend more money? Music creates an emotional connection with shoppers and has been shown to affect how people move through the store. The more people linger in the store, the more they buy! The world is sending us messages and often, we are not even aware of how they affect our lives.

We certainly cannot go live under a rock and ignore what is happening in the world around us, but if we are not careful, we can begin to believe the lies this world tries to sell us. If we are not careful, our minds can be influenced in the wrong way and can be filled up with garbage.

Many mornings before my eyes are fully open from sleep, I find myself singing song lyrics in my thoughts. I wonder if that ever happens to you. How does that happen? It happens because the music we listen to takes up residence in our brains such that even our subconscious knows the lyrics. The music we listen to takes up space in our hearts and minds. Our hearts connect to the lyrics and our brains remember the words. Music affects our attitudes and even the choices we make. Music is powerful and I've learned I need to be careful about what music I choose to listen to.

The books we read affect us too because we imagine ourselves in the storyline. This can lead to feeling as if our lives are subpar and ordinary. Reading a romance novel may be enjoyable, but if our marriage is not in a healthy place, reading a romance novel may cause damage to our marriage. We might begin thinking things like, "My husband would never treat me that nice," or, "I wish I had a husband who would take me away on an island vacation."

If we are not careful, even the television shows and movies we watch can sweep our minds away to desire a more exciting life. They can cause us to feel as if our lives or the people in our lives are inadequate. Depending on our current season of life, seemingly innocent habits may cause us to look for joy in people, places, and other things besides looking for joy in Jesus. Satan is looking for a place to get a foothold in your life and he likes to sneak in when you least expect it. Keep in mind the choices you make in music, books, movies, TV shows, etc., can lead to feelings of discontentment, lust, jealousy, greed, anger and worry. It is important to pay attention to any place Satan tries to trip you up. He is looking to steal your joy so be careful not to give him any room. The Bible tells us Satan comes to do three detrimental things in our lives:

The thief comes only to steal and kill and destroy; I have come that they may have life, and have it to the full.
˜John 10:10

Satan is sneaky in his approach. Little by little, we form habits that open us up to Satan's schemes. We must be alert and aware of what he is doing, and then we must put up guardrails to safeguard our lives.

Be alert and of sober mind. Your enemy the devil prowls around like a roaring lion looking for someone to devour.
˜1 Peter 5:8

Be on your guard; stand firm in the faith;
be courageous; be strong.
˜1 Corinthians 16:13

In His Word, God also warns us about how we handle our hearts. Our hearts are critical when it comes to our thoughts.

Above all else, guard your heart,
for everything you do flows from it.
˜Proverbs 4:23

This word, "heart" is defined as the center of who we are, our intellect, our will, our inner person. The mind and heart are strongly connected and they align tightly with our thoughts and feelings. The Bible tells us the hearts of men are evil. It is out of a person's heart that sinful thoughts come into our minds. These sinful thoughts lead to sinful actions.

For it is from within, out of a person's heart, that evil thoughts come—sexual immorality, theft, murder, adultery, greed, malice, deceit, lewdness, envy, slander, arrogance and folly. All these evils come from inside and defile a person."
~Mark 7:21-23

For from the heart come evil thoughts, murder, adultery, all sexual immorality, theft, lying, and slander.
~Matthew 15:19

The heart is more deceitful than all else and is desperately sick; who can understand it?
~Jeremiah 17:9

man's sinful heart   sinful thought   dwelling on this sinful thought   sinful action

When a sinful idea comes into our minds, we have a choice to make. Will we dwell on it or will we replace it with something good? Will we begin to act on it, or will we confess it and change the channel in our minds? It is in the life of our minds that sin is decided. We make up our minds first, and then we act. Isn't this strategy exactly what Satan did in the Garden of Eden with Adam and Eve? He placed a sinful thought into their minds by placing doubt into their hearts. Satan planted a seed of confusion into their minds about what

God said. He wanted them to question who God is and what God said.

Now the serpent was more crafty than any of the wild animals the LORD God had made. He said to the woman, "Did God really say, 'You must not eat from any tree in the garden'?"
~Genesis 3:1

Satan is up to his same old tricks today. He wants us to be confused about the truth of God. That's why he works so hard to keep you and me away from church, reading our Bibles, and joining Bible studies. He does not want us to know the truth. Satan knows when we read and understand God's Word, it is much harder for him to trick us into believing his lies. When we don't make time to read God's Word, we will never know truth.

Your battle with worry and anxiety is a battle with Satan. He wants to occupy your mind with fear, lies, and confusion. He wants to destroy your relationships, your family, and your integrity. He wants to steal your confidence in God and your joy. He often uses what we think is an innocent habit to stir up sinful thoughts and attitudes. This encourages us to drift away from God. Satan knows if he can cause our minds to become distracted with earthly things, he can prevent us from living the joyful life God intends for us to live. The good news is we can fight back against his schemes.

When we see Satan at work in our lives, we need to pray and ask God to help us change that area in our lives so we do not give Satan an open door. We can also be more alert as to what we are thinking. It is so important that we pay close attention to our thought life and our hearts. We need to do what Jesus told us to do - be on guard! When anxious, negative, ungodly thoughts try to move into our head space, we need to kick those thoughts out and choose to focus on things that align with God's Word. We have the power to change the channel. You really do have the power to reclaim your thoughts, but it takes awareness and practice. You and I can create new habits in our lives that help us fight back against the schemes of Satan who wants to destroy us.

With God's help, your life can be transformed by the renewing of your mind. Watching and guarding your thought life is vital to overcoming worry and anxiety. Watching and guarding your thoughts is vital to living a joy-filled life!

I love this phrase below. Although scholars disagree about who originally said it, I think it is powerful and true:

> Watch your thoughts; they become words.
> Watch your words; they become actions.
> Watch your actions; they become habit.
> Watch your habits; they become character.
> Watch your character; it becomes your destiny.

LOVING GOD WITH YOUR MIND.

As we work to reclaim our thoughts, we also need to understand the importance of loving God with our minds. God is love. The only way we know how to love is because God first loved us. Love is powerful. It is the greatest of all things.

> *And now these three remain: faith, hope, and love.*
> *But the greatest of these is love.*
> *~1 Corinthians 13:13*

Our God is a holy and righteous God, and He is also a jealous God. He is jealous *for* us! We are to love Him, first.

You shall have no other gods before me. You shall not make for yourself an image in the form of anything in heaven above or on the earth beneath or in the waters below. You shall not bow down to them or worship them; for I, the Lord your God, am a jealous God, punishing the children for the sin of the parents to the third and fourth generation of those who hate me.
~Exodus 20:3-5

Loving God first is the greatest commandment. In the Gospel of Mark, Jesus was tested by one of the teachers of the law when he asked Jesus which of the commandments was the most important. Here is how Jesus answered:

"The most important one," answered Jesus, "is this: 'Hear, O Israel: The Lord our God, the Lord is one. Love the Lord your God with all your heart and with all your soul and with all your mind and with all your strength.' The second is this: 'Love your neighbor as yourself.' There is no commandment greater than these."
~Mark 12:29-31

As you and I reclaim our thoughts, we need to keep in mind that we are commanded to love God with all of who we are, and that includes our minds. Let us understand fully that this is not a suggestion. This is a commandment.

Have you ever thought about what it means to love God with your mind? What does that look like? I have learned in order for me to love God with my mind, I need to think about the things of God. I need to spend time in His Word. God wants me to use the intellect He gave me to know Him more. This means I need to use my judgment and reasoning to think critically about the things of God. God is all-knowing and He knows my innermost thoughts. He desires not only for my actions to demonstrate love for Him but also my thoughts. One way you and I love God with our minds is to take captive every thought we have to Jesus.

We demolish arguments and every pretension that
sets itself up against the knowledge of God, and we
take captive every thought to make it
obedient to Christ.
~2 Corinthians 10:5

The context of this verse uses an image of war - where an enemy would be caught and taken away. I like this imagery because it reminds me that we are at war with our enemy, Satan, and his battlefield is our minds. He knows if he can sneak attack our thoughts, he has us right where he wants us...fearful and worried.

To take captive every thought means we need to get serious about taking charge of what we think about. Any thought that comes into our mind that is against God's Word needs to be captured and exiled from our thought life. Satan does not want us to study or know God's Word. When we know truth, Satan knows his days of influence in our lives are numbered. He knows we are set free by the truth of God's Word.

As you and I become more aware of what we are thinking about, we will start to recognize how Satan brings worry and fear into our thought lives. As we practice taking those thoughts captive to Christ, the landscape of our minds will become more godly. As our thoughts align more and more with the truth of God's Word, peace and joy will take root and worry and fear will dissipate.

Let's revisit the example of getting ready in the mornings. As Satan begins to hurl insults at me:

Damaging thought: You look old and tired. Your skin is also flabby and saggy. You should feel bad about yourself.

Reclaiming my thoughts: The Bible says I am fearfully and wonderfully made. It also says that beauty fades away, but a woman who honors the LORD deserves to be praised. Age is a gift! I still have a heartbeat and that means Jesus is not done with me!

Satan likes to remind us of our sin, and he likes to remind us of our flaws. He also wants us to feel dissatisfied with other people in our lives. He wants to remind you of what is wrong with the people you love. He wants to destroy your relationships. If he can make you feel disappointed with other people, he knows you might pull away from those important relationships.

Don't let him win! Fight back by recognizing his schemes and then change the channel in your mind. Instead of thinking about all of the things that are wrong with other people, focus on what is right with them! Make a list of what you love about them! What are their good qualities? Choose to be grateful and remember - no person, church, workplace, or home is perfect. We are all sinful, flawed people and we need Jesus.

A PRACTICAL EXAMPLE

Years ago, I felt God convict me about my thought life. On the outside, maybe my life looked okay, but on the inside, I struggled with having judgmental thoughts and these thoughts did not please God. When I had a judging thought about someone, I would ignore it and not consider it sinful because it never led me to evil actions. God laid it heavy on my heart that He searches my heart and mind and even my thoughts matter to Him. In order for us to reclaim our thoughts and love God with our minds, we need to examine what we are thinking about. Let's consider this practical example:

When you go shopping and you see someone who is not "put together," what do you think? If someone looks dirty, has on pajamas in the middle of the day, and is acting loud and obnoxious, what thoughts go through your mind? Ask yourself this question: Do I criticize or judge people secretly in my thoughts?

Maybe like me, you do not want to admit what you may think about this person. I confess my thoughts are not always aligned with God's Word. My first thought is not that this person is made in the image of God (James 3:9) and is fearfully and wonderfully made (Psalm 139:14). When I search my heart, disappointedly I see my thoughts are often judgmental and prideful.

Another question to consider is this - what thoughts do you have when you see someone you do not like? Maybe someone has mistreated you or someone in your family. How do you respond to that person? I can be quick to make assumptions about someone based on their appearance or their previous behavior toward me. From the outside, my words and actions seem kind, but my private thoughts are not.

God commands us to love Him with our minds and He commands us to love others (including those who do not love us back). He knows every thought you and I have. He knows all of our sinful internal thoughts. We cannot hide our sinful thoughts from Him.

Loving God with our minds requires us to be honest and humble. It also requires a repentant spirit. Being aware of my sinful thoughts was a life-changing concept for me. When I realized God does not only care about my actions, but He also cares about what I am thinking about, it changed the way I looked at my sin. Why had it taken me so long to figure this out? I think it's because I knew my thought life was private, and outwardly, I was pretty good at doing the polite thing. Many of us are good at thinking one thing but behaving another way. Out of politeness, we can seem kind and nice when we encounter someone we do not like, but in our minds, we have thoughts that are not pleasing to God. Let me give you an example of something that happened to me - also, no real names are being used in this story.

Years ago, Bryan and I moved to a new town and there was a lady in my community who didn't like me. At least, that's how it felt to me. Let's call her Barbara. I tried to be nice to Barbara, going out of my way to say hello when I would see her. Each time I tried to speak to her, it felt like she was not interested in having a conversation with me. I know how to take a hint, so after several attempts to make friends with Barbara, I stopped going out of my way to speak to her. If you have ever moved to a new town, you know how hard it can be to make new friends, especially when you're an adult. You're not from the area and you don't know anyone. You want to belong, but you don't feel like you belong. You are a transplant in a new community and it can feel lonely. That's how I felt. I was looking for godly women to connect with. I was looking for friendship, but it was obvious Barbara was not interested in being my friend. When I examined my heart, this cold shoulder from Barbara bothered me. I wondered why she disliked me. Why did she not want to be my friend?

A few months went by and I was at a community event. I overheard one of Barbara's friends make a comment to a group of ladies about something Barbara said. I was sitting close by and could hear their conversation. I heard my name come up in their conversation. Barbara had made a negative comment about me and her friend was talking about it to a group of women.

STOP THE BUS - what in the world is going on? Why am I the topic of this conversation? I know we should be able to put on our big girl panties and let things like this go. Things like this are petty and not worth our emotional energy. It's not really a big deal, right? Well, for me, it hit me hard. Maybe it was because my family had moved to another state and I already felt out of place. Maybe it was because I had started a new job and was emotionally exhausted. Maybe it was because I had left all of my close friends behind when we moved and I was longing for friendship. Regardless of why it hit me so hard, my feelings were hurt, and I felt worried that I might not find good friends in this new community.

It wasn't long after I overheard this conversation that I saw Barbara out to eat at a restaurant. That particular day had not been the best day for me, and when I saw Barbara out of the corner of my eye, I thought of things in my mind that were not kind (and I may have rolled my eyes just a little).

When I spotted Barbara, I pretended not to see her. I kept my eyes down, looking at the menu as she walked past me. I was intensely studying that menu and did not look her way, but she saw me and she politely said, "Hey Joy, how are you?" I faked a surprised look on my face as if I had just now noticed her, and then I smiled. I said with a sweet, but fake tone in my voice, "Fine, Barbara, how are you...it's so good to see you."

I lied.

It was not, in fact, good to see her. Not at all. Quite honestly, I would have rather been having a root canal than making small talk with Barbara. My feelings were hurt by what she said about me and in my humanness, I was not thinking nice thoughts. Barbara did not know what I was really thinking, but I knew...and so did God.

Can you relate to how I felt? Have you ever had someone say something bad about you and then you later found out about it? How did it make you feel? Did it cause you to worry, feel alone, or rejected? I felt all of those things. Maybe you can relate to how I responded to Barbara. Maybe like me, you have also had an encounter where you faked being kind, but on the inside, you were not thinking kind thoughts.

My actions were nice and polite, but what if Barbara knew what I was really thinking about her? What if she really knew what was in my heart? What if each of us had our own personal teleprompter that followed us around displaying our inner thoughts for all to see? That would be terrible wouldn't it? It would reveal the sin inside our hearts. I'm glad there is no teleprompter displaying my thoughts to the world because sometimes I am ashamed of my thoughts.

When we have sinful thoughts, we often do not tell another soul. We keep them secret, safely tucked away in the life of our minds. No one is a mind reader so no one knows what we are really thinking. It's pretty easy to dismiss or ignore a secret sin that only exists in our minds. Satan wants us to believe that as long as our thoughts do not lead to sinful actions, they are not a big deal. This is *not* true. God cares about our thoughts and if we want to love Him with our minds, we need to recognize the sin that exists inside our minds.

God's Word tells us that our thoughts matter and He knows every private and secret thought. He knows everything.

If our hearts condemn us, we know that God is greater than our hearts, and he knows everything.
~1 John 3:20

"You have heard that it was said, 'You shall not commit adultery.' But I tell you that anyone who looks at a woman lustfully has already committed adultery with her in his heart"
~Matthew 5:27-28

In my encounter with Barbara, my thoughts were not pleasing to God. In my mind, I judged Barbara. I had ugly thoughts about her and I made assumptions about her based on something someone else said. I realized I needed to change.

If you and I want to stop thinking about things that make us feel worried, we need to love God with our minds. We need to create a thought life that honors God and gives no room for Satan. This means we must examine what we are thinking about. Instead of ignoring sinful thoughts, we need to talk to God about them. Let's get into a habit of confessing our sinful thoughts to God and asking Him for forgiveness.

As you seek to love God with your mind, what sinful thoughts do you need to confess to Him?

_____

_____

_____

_____

_____

As you begin to be more aware of your thoughts, maybe like me, you will find that you also make assumptions and judgments about other people. If so, I encourage you to work on breaking that habit. Be aware of how it displeases God and ask Him to help you love Him better with your mind.

The mind governed by the flesh is death, but the mind governed by the Spirit is life and peace.
~Romans 8:6

TOOLS TO RECLAIM YOUR THOUGHTS

It can be hard to change what you are thinking about. Reclaiming your thoughts takes practice. It doesn't happen overnight. In my personal journey, there are several tools I have used to help me take back control of my thought life. One tool I have used to reclaim my thought life is the "RED X" tool.

The enemy whispers negative, damaging thoughts to you and me every day. He works hard to attack your mind because he knows if he can get your thoughts off of the things of God, he has a chance of preventing you from living out your God-given callings. Satan wants you to feel defeated and hopeless, but you don't have to listen to him. The RED X tool has helped me stop negative, self-degrading thoughts from taking up residence in my mind. I hope it helps you too!

THE RED X TOOL

 The RED X tool is simple but it is powerful. It takes practice, but I have used it for years. It has helped me reclaim my thoughts and fight back against worry. Here's how it works.

86

When I feel worried, and a damaging thought (or image) comes to my mind, I quickly recognize it as worry getting the best of me. To fight back, I simply close my eyes and imagine drawing a big red X over the image in my mind. Then, I imagine myself breaking through the image and destroying it. This stops me from focusing on the thought or image. It redirects my thoughts to focus on something better. I often say out loud, "I am not going to think about this." It seems so simple, but for me, it has been incredibly effective. When negative, damaging thoughts come to your mind, you can take action to stop yourself from dwelling on them. This will help you form better mental habits. Negative thoughts often repeat themselves, so by canceling them out quickly, you redirect your focus to something that aligns with God's truth.

This tool can also be helpful when a sinful or dishonoring thought comes into your mind. When you think thoughts that are unkind or selfish, recognize those thoughts as temptation from Satan and quickly cancel them out with a big red X. This will help clear your mind of Satan's attacks and it will keep your mind fixed on the things of God.

FIGHT TOOL

Another tool that has been helpful to me when I have struggled with worrisome thoughts is the FIGHT tool. What I love about this tool is that I can use it anytime and anywhere, even when I am driving down the highway.

When I feel attacked with worrisome thoughts, I use this tool to remind me of what is true. I use it to replace my negative, damaging thoughts with ones that are godly. This tool uses the word, FIGHT, as a way to remember what to say and do.

When a wave of fear comes over me and I begin to dwell on the bad things that might happen, I start to work through the FIGHT tool. I go through each letter and remind myself of what is true. Below is a basic outline of things you can say out loud when you feel Satan attacking your mind.

F: FEAR IS JUST A FEELING.

I'm feeling afraid right now about something bad that might happen. Fear is just a feeling - it has no power over me. I feel afraid but that's because my body is responding to this situation exactly the way God designed it to. My stress hormones and chemicals are working and they are making me feel this way. My heart rate is up and my blood pressure is too, but that is normal when you're afraid. I know these feelings of worry and fear will go away. They always go away. Fear is nothing more than a feeling.

I: IMMEDIATELY RESPOND BY TRUSTING IN GOD.

Although I feel afraid and worried right now, I am in control of how I will respond in this situation. I will immediately respond by choosing to trust in God. I am choosing to stay calm because I know He is with me. My feelings are just feelings. They have no power over me. God is in control of my destiny and no matter what happens, I choose to trust in Him.

G: GO TO GOD.

Satan is using fear against me right now, but I will not panic. I know God is greater than Satan and God is on my side. I belong to Him. Instead of panicking or dwelling on these negative thoughts, I am choosing to go to God in prayer. My worried thoughts are making me think about what might happen. Instead of worrying about the "what ifs," I am going to talk with God about how I feel. He is my Helper. He is my Provider. He is my Savior. I will pray and trust Him to help me as only He can!

H: HAVE COURAGE.

Right now, I am choosing to have courage. No matter what happens, I know God is good and that He loves me. Even if something really bad happens to me, I know I do not face my trials alone. God is with me. He promises to never leave me. Having courage means I move forward in spite of feeling afraid. I have no reason to fear because God is with me.

T: THOUGHT CHECK.

Right now, I am choosing to take every thought captive to Christ. My thoughts are spinning out of control, but I am going to stop and breathe deeply. I am going to examine my thoughts. Are they true? Are they right? Do they honor God? I am going to replace my anxious thoughts with the truth of God's Word. Right now, I am also choosing to have a grateful heart. Thank you, God for loving me. Thank you for being a faithful God. I am grateful for all You do for me.

I encourage you to use this FIGHT tool when you have a wave of fearful, worrisome thoughts come over you. Speak these truths out loud. Speak Bible verses out loud to help settle your mind. Remember that worry is unpredictable, and it often comes when you least expect it. The FIGHT tool is a great way to remember how to *fight* the feelings of excessive worry with the truth of God's Word. I have also found the FIGHT tool helpful when a panic attack happens.

Have you ever experienced a panic attack?

Panic attacks can be terrifying, especially when you have one for the first time and you do not know what is happening to you. A panic attack is an experience of intense fear that comes on suddenly. It often happens when there is no real danger. A panic attack can make someone feel like they are losing control of their life, and sometimes they feel like they are dying. A panic attack triggers physical symptoms that mimic a heart attack. You may be surprised to know how many people show up in the emergency room thinking they are having a heart attack, only to find out it is a panic attack.

Panic attacks bring feelings of impending doom or gloom. It feels like a wave of fear is overtaking you. They happen when you least expect it, and symptoms include:

- shaking
- increased heart rate
- sweating
- feeling intense fear
- numbness
- shortness of breath
- nausea

Medical studies show that panic attacks occur in an overwhelmingly large percentage of people who survive a traumatic experience. I experienced my first panic attack after my tornado experience. It occurred many weeks after the tornado hit my house. I had no idea what was happening to me. All of a sudden, I had a wave of fear come over me and I felt like I was dying. When it started, I was driving. I pulled over onto the side of the road. I was sure I was having a heart attack. I did my best to stay calm and pull myself together, but all I could do was cry and worry. I was shaking, and felt very nervous. I was so scared. I prayed, and over and over again, I asked God to help me. If you have ever experienced a panic attack, you know how it makes you feel completely out of control. It is a terrifying experience!

After this experience, I began researching panic attacks, and I realized there were strategies and tools I could use to help me. I did not have to allow this to overtake my life. This is when I learned the importance of using self-talk. When a wave of gloom and doom came over me, instead of focusing on how I was feeling, I started speaking truth to myself. I reminded myself that this feeling was only worry and anxiety getting the best of me. I reminded myself that Satan wanted me to fall apart and be fearful. I reminded myself that a panic attack is not life-threatening. I told myself that these feelings of fear would go away as I breathed and prayed.

Over time, I developed the FIGHT tool, and it helped me overcome the effects of feeling fearful and panicked. The more I practiced using the FIGHT tool, the less panic I experienced. Over time, my panic attacks completely subsided.

PUTTING THESE TOOLS INTO PRACTICE

The FIGHT and RED X tools help to combat the "what if" disease of worry. When you begin thinking about all of the bad things that might happen, use these tools to cancel out your damaging thoughts. Replace your thoughts with godly ones. It will take practice and it won't happen overnight, but the more you practice using these tools to keep your mind focused on truth, the less you will struggle with excessive worry.

Whenever a wave of fear comes over you, quickly recognize that feeling as a spirit of fear from Satan. Remind yourself that with God's help, you have the power to fight back. Utilize the strategies and tools we have covered in this section. Control your inner voice, change the channel, write down Bible verses on sticky notes, examine your habits, love God with your mind, and implement the RED X and FIGHT tools.

In the movie, Karate Kid, Daniel did the work Mr. Miyagi instructed him to do. He practiced painting the fence, painting the house, sanding the floors, and waxing the cars. He created good habits while doing the work and this conditioned his body to respond when Mr. Miyagi used karate against Daniel. Those ingrained new habits helped Daniel respond in just the right way.

Similar to Daniel, you can learn how to overcome worry by doing the work God's way. By practicing these strategies and tools we have covered, you will retrain your mind to think about things that are pleasing to God. It takes time. It takes work. It even takes discipline to stick with it, but the more you practice, the more your mind will be free from worry and anxiety. You have control over what thoughts you allow to take up residence in your mind. By taking back control of your thought life, you can find joy again!

A Prescription for Joy
STEP THREE

Name _____

Date _____

Practice using the RED X Tool

Memorize the steps of the FIGHT Tool

Memorize Philippians 4:8-9

Practice changing the channel on your negative thoughts

Write scripture on sticky notes and place them where you will see them each day

_____   Dr. Joy

Date   Signature

A prayer for reclaiming your thoughts

God, worry steals my joy. It makes me feel helpless and defenseless. I know these feelings are not true. Your Word is truth and I know You are able. There is nothing impossible for You. Will You help me examine my thoughts and change the channel inside my worried mind? Please help me use the strategies and tools I learned in this section to overcome worrisome and fearful thoughts. Help me fight back against Satan's schemes as I develop new, positive habits in my mind. I love You. I need You. Amen.

Be on your guard; stand firm in the faith;
be courageous; be strong.
~1 Corinthians 16:13

Thoughts from Step Three

Take a few minutes to write down what encouraged you from this section. What main points do you want to remember and use in your life?

_____

_____

_____

_____

_____

_____

_____

_____

_____

_____

_____

_____

_____

_____

_____

_____

_____

_____

_____

_____

GRATEFUL JOURNALING

Reclaiming our thoughts requires that we replace the negative thoughts filling up our minds with ones that are good, right, true, and from God. Keeping a gratitude journal is a great way to keep your mind focused on the goodness of God.

Studies have shown that many people who keep a gratitude journal are overall happier and healthier. They tend to sleep better and even have improved relationships.

I encourage you, my friend, to start keeping a gratitude journal. Find a journal you can designate strictly for journaling about gratitude. Keep this journal on your nightstand beside your bed. Before you go to bed each night, grab your journal and answer these questions:

- What happened today that brought me joy?
- What five things am I grateful for today and why?
- How has God blessed my life?
- What are three things that made me smile today?
- Where did I see God at work today?

After you finish journaling, pray and thank God for His goodness and how He has blessed your life.

RED X TOOL

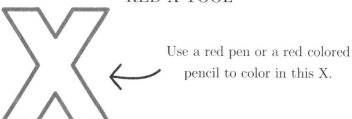

Use a red pen or a red colored pencil to color in this X.

Pay attention to your inner voice. Quickly recognize worrisome and damaging thoughts (or images). Remind yourself those are not from God. Close your eyes and imagine drawing a big red X over the image in your mind. Then, imagine yourself breaking through the image and destroying it. Once that thought or image leaves your mind, quickly redirect your thoughts to focus on something that is in line with what the Bible says. It may be helpful to speak out loud something like this as you draw the red X over the image in your mind:

"I am not going to think about this terrible thing. This thought is a lie from Satan! I will not allow myself to think or dwell on this. I know God loves me. I know He is with me. I can trust in Him no matter what."

The FIGHT Tool
(a quick reminder)

F Fear is just a feeling: My body is responding exactly how God created it to respond when I feel afraid. This feeling will go away. It always goes away.

I Immediately respond by trusting in God: I am going to face the fear I am feeling. I realize it has no power over me. I am choosing to trust in God.

G Go to God: I will not panic. I am going to go to God about this right now in prayer. I will talk with Him about how I feel because I know He loves me.

H Have courage: I am choosing to have courage. God is with me. He will help me. Fear will not stop me. I will keep moving forward in spite of how I feel.

T Thought check: My thoughts are not lining up with truth right now. I am going to get my mind off of these negative thoughts and start thinking about what I know is true. I will also think about what I am grateful for and I will thank God.

Step Four

RELEASE
CONTROL

GOD IS IN CONTROL
OVER ALL THINGS

Step Four: Release Control

I know it is hard to imagine, but we once lived in a world without the Internet. It used to be much harder to find information. There was no such thing as shopping online or looking for ideas on websites. When women needed ideas for decorating their homes, instead of searching for photos online, they subscribed to home magazines and shopped storefront windows.

I remember my mom subscribing to a few home magazines that would arrive at our house each month so she could stay up-to-date on the latest decorating trends. She was one of the best homemakers around. She knew the art of making a house into a home. No matter what crafty project she set her mind to, she conquered it beautifully.

One thing my mom always wanted to try her hand at was pottery, so one year for Christmas, I gifted her with a mother/daughter day at the pottery studio. When we arrived, we were given an apron to wear to protect our clothes and the instructor gave us a lump of clay.

He sat down at the potter's wheel and instructed the class on how to "throw a pot." A lump of clay was centered on the wheel, and he used a sponge to wet the clay as he began to spin the potter's wheel. He explained the importance of using only a little water as you shape the clay. Too much water may cause a big mess.

While the wheel was spinning, he showed us how to mold the clay. It was a tedious process. When the consistency of the clay was just right, he showed us how to pull up the sides of the clay to form a piece of pottery. From my perspective, it looked fairly easy, and I felt pretty confident I could make something beautiful.

Wet the clay, spin the wheel, "throw" a beautiful piece of pottery, and create a family heirloom. Got it!

As I sat down at the wheel with my lump of clay, it did not take long for me to realize I had completely overestimated my ability to create a family heirloom.

I placed the clay on the center of the wheel and wet the sponge. I squeezed the sponge to wet the clay as I pressed down the foot pedal to start the wheel spinning. In my excitement, I pressed the foot pedal down way too hard and the wheel started spinning at what looked like 60 miles per hour. I panicked as I looked around in hopes that no one was watching. I kept thinking, "Where is the brake on this thing?" Having no idea what I was doing, I went to grab the clay and somehow, it turned loose from the wheel, and took flight.

Completely mortified, I jumped up and quickly pulled the mushy glob of clay off the floor and put it back on the wheel. I had been working for less than five minutes and I already had mud in my hair and on my face. It was a good thing I was wearing that apron. I questioned my giftedness at pottery-making and raised my hand to ask for a new lump of clay. As I waited for help, I looked over and saw my mom. She was sitting at the wheel, and I noticed her wheel was spinning at a reasonable speed. She looked so calm...and pristine, not one drop of wet clay on her. I watched as she gently squeezed a little water on top of the clay to soften it up and she began working it in her hands. She seemed to have no trouble keeping the clay centered on the wheel. After a few minutes, I watched with amazement as she lifted up the sides of the clay to form a little bowl. I wondered if she had been secretly taking pottery classes without me because even the instructor commented on how well she was doing. There I was looking like I had wrestled a bunch of pigs in the mud and my mom was making a family heirloom.

I want you to keep this image of a potter working at a potter's wheel fresh in your mind as we continue this journey of overcoming worry. Imagine in your mind a potter sitting down at the potter's wheel with an ugly lump of clay. The potter decides what to make out of that lump of clay. The potter has a plan for the clay. The potter is in control over the process. The clay is not in control. In the book of Jeremiah, we find these verses:

This is the word that came to Jeremiah from the Lord: "Go down to the potter's house, and there I will give you my message." So I went down to the potter's house, and I saw him working at the wheel. But the pot he was shaping from the clay was marred in his hands; so the potter formed it into another pot, shaping it as seemed best to him.
~~Jeremiah 18:1-4

The fourth step in overcoming excessive worry is to learn how to release control. Raise your hand if you like to be in control. Raise your hand if you are a detailed planner.

Do you like a plan? Do you like to know what is going to happen next? Do you feel worried when things do not go according to your plans?

To be in control means:

- You have the power to influence or direct people's behavior or events.
- You determine the behavior or supervise the running of something.

Confession: I like to be in control.

It is normal for you to want to control things in your life. Feeling in control brings a sense of power, certainty, and predictability. It brings consistency into your life, and it helps you feel like you are managing your life well.

When I think about being in control of my life, there are three things that come to mind:

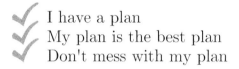 I have a plan
My plan is the best plan
Don't mess with my plan

How do you feel about making a plan and sticking to it? I think most of us like to make a plan and we want things to go according to that plan. As long as life follows our plan, we feel comfortable.

Having a plan is good. There is nothing wrong with having a plan. In fact, we find scripture that mentions the value of planning and preparing ahead.

The plans of the diligent lead surely to abundance, but everyone who is hasty comes only to poverty.
~Proverbs 21:5

It is almost impossible for us to manage our lives without some sort of plan. There is a problem, however, when our plans take little consideration of God's will. When we make life plans without consulting God, we are in the danger zone of being outside of God's will. It is important that we prayerfully make plans that align with God's Word. It is also important that we hold on to our plans loosely.

The funny thing about plans is they do not always work out. Take your thoughts back to when you were 16 years old. Did you write down your plans and dreams? How did you see your life going? Make a few notes below about what your life's plans were when you were 16. What were your goals and dreams?

_____

_____

_____

_____

_____

_____

_____

_____

_____

_____

_____

Maybe your life's plans were similar to mine. Marry the man of your dreams, have beautiful, highly intelligent, God-fearing children, make lots of money, and have a beautiful home. You can even throw in the white picket fence and the dog in the back yard...and there you have the American dream! Let's all live happily ever after! Except, this is not how everyone's story unfolds.

When you fast-forward to your life now, did everything turn out exactly the way you planned?

Probably not.

The reality is life is hard. Dreams do not always come true. Our lives do not always turn out the way we plan. At the age of 16, no one plans on being divorced by the time they are 40. No one hopes for cancer. No one dreams of financial hardship. No one desires to have strained relationships with their family. No one wishes for a tragic accident to change their lives forever. Our hopes, dreams, and plans are usually full of happiness, health, wealth, and comfort. No one dreams of a broken heart.

When life does not go according to our plans, we feel like we have lost control. Just like my lump of clay on the potter's wheel, life sometimes spins out of control and goes in a direction we did not plan for it to go. We do not have the power to control every situation. We also do not have the power to control other people. People in our lives make decisions that hurt us and it can be difficult knowing how to respond. I do not need to tell you that life is not a fairytale. Sometimes life hurts, and when hurtful things happen, a cloud of worry can surround us. Hopelessness can set in.

We know worry is a joy-stealer, and Satan uses it to prevent us from living the life God intended for us to live. We know worry is not from God but until we understand what causes us to worry, we may find ourselves trapped in a vicious cycle, not knowing how to escape.

In Step One we walked through the gripping effects of fear, and we learned worry is rooted in fear. Fear is often the starting point of, "The Cycle of Worry."

The Cycle of Worry is a pattern we can find ourselves in when life takes an unexpected turn. The Cycle of Worry typically begins to spin out of an underlying fear. Worry is rooted in fear. The driving forces of worry are the small circles inside The Cycle of Worry. These are the engines that keep fear and worry alive. The more engines that are spinning, the more worry takes over our lives.

If we are able to identify what we are afraid of, and then understand how to trust God with that fear, we can begin to stop this cycle from spinning out of control. As we look into our hearts to find what is driving these engines of worry, we can put the brakes on The Cycle of Worry. Identifying stress and triggers, examining our "what if" thoughts, and understanding our body's alert response helps us manage our worry better. The more we understand, the better chance we have of stopping this cycle from overtaking our lives.

When an unexpected problem triggers a fearful thought to take root, our alert system kicks into gear. As we begin to feel worried, our minds become consumed with the "what ifs." Thoughts of what might happen plunge us into deeper worry and then we realize we are losing control of things in our lives. We start to feel the physical symptoms of stress (increased heart rate, shakiness, increased blood pressure, fast breathing, etc). Suffering from physical symptoms of worry makes us feel even more fearful and the cycle continues to spin. It is hard to break free.

The need to control things in our lives causes the Cycle of Worry to spin out of control. Learning to release this desire to be in control can be one of the most powerful, life-changing things we ever do. But how do we release control? It starts with surrendering to the One who is in control over all things...God.

When I was a senior in high school, I remember a speaker saying, "You can be anything you want to be. You can do anything you want to do. If you can dream it, you can do it!" It was inspirational and I still remember people cheering loudly and standing to their feet as he finished his speech. He helped us believe we could do and be anything! Many years later, I now know that although he gave a riveting speech, his statements were not entirely true. You and I cannot do anything *we* want to do. We cannot be anything *we* want to be. I will never be Miss America. I will never dunk a basketball on a regulation-sized goal...without the help of a ladder. I will never walk on the moon. But do you know what I can do? Do you know who I can be? I can live the life my Creator planned for me to live. I can be who He created me to be! It is important that you and I understand the truth about who God is. He loves us and He cares for us. He is involved in the details of our lives. There are two words I want us to explore that will help us understand how God oversees the circumstances of our lives. Those words are sovereignty and providence.

The Bible teaches that God is sovereign, but what exactly does that mean? The word sovereign means authority. The Hebrew word means royalty, royal power, reign, and kingdom.

The LORD has established His throne in the heavens;
and His sovereignty rules over all.
~Psalm 103:19

God is sovereign and that means He rules over all things. He has given man the freedom to make choices, but in all things, God never loses control over His greater plan. He directs all things to fulfill His perfect plan. Although we do not fully understand why He allows bad things to happen, we know He is mighty in power, and He is ruler over all. He is working all things together for something good, and we can have confidence that no one can stop our God.

"But if it is from God, you will not be able to stop
these men; you will only find yourselves
fighting against God."
~Acts 5:39

What about the word providence? Providence means "the protective care of God." God cares and provides for His creation. He is active in our lives, and He makes provisions for us. God has foreknowledge and foresight. He is always at work, often behind the scenes, accomplishing His perfect will.

He is involved in our lives, going before us and guiding us to where we need to be.

The LORD of Hosts Himself has planned it; therefore, who can stand in its way? It is His hand that is outstretched, so who can turn it back?
~Isaiah 14:27

When we understand God is all-knowing and powerful, we have a better understanding that He created us with a purpose in mind. He is active in the details of our lives, and He guides our steps. Often, I have made plans and then prayed and asked God to bless my plans. I wonder if you have ever done that. My friend, what would happen if we changed our approach? What if we first ask God to have *His* way and will in our lives? What if we first seek out *His* plan instead of our own? He made us. He knows who He made us to be and what He made us to do. Now...we want to put this in its proper perspective. God gave us a brain and He gave us intellect to use. He wants us to make plans, but He first wants us to surrender ourselves to His will. He is the One who determines our steps.

We can make our plans, but the LORD determines our steps.
~Proverbs 16:9

In the mother/daughter day pottery class I attended, my mom made a little bowl out of her clay, while my lump of clay became nothing useful. Clay can become something beautiful but only when it is in the hands of a skilled potter. It is the potter who molds the clay into something useful and beautiful.

The clay does not mold itself.

As you think about this concept of fully releasing control of your life to God, it is good to trace the hand of God in your life. Take some time to reflect on how God has directed your steps in the past. What has He done in your life, specifically, to guide you to where He wanted you to be? Think about how much you trust God. You and I need to check our hearts when it comes to our future. Do we believe God has our best interest in mind? Do we believe we can trust Him to lead the way, even when bad things happen?

We cannot become anything we want to be, but we can become everything God desires us to be when we give ourselves over fully to Him. He is the potter, and we are the clay. When we yield to Him, He lovingly shapes us into the person He wants us to be. Isn't it amazing that God had a plan for your life even before you were born? He is all-knowing and you can trust that He knows what He is doing.

As we continue to work through our worry, what we need is for God's peace to take up residence in our hearts and minds. He is the giver of the peace and contentment our hearts and minds need, but in order to find the peace we are searching for, we must give Him all of who we are.

Yet you, LORD, are our Father. We are the clay, you
are the potter; we are all the work of your hand.
~Isaiah 64:8

Before moving forward in this section, I want to encourage you to take some time to journal. I have provided a few questions on the next page for you to answer that relate to control and surrender. Grab your journal and a pen and write your thoughts and feelings to the questions. Before you begin, pray and ask God to help you answer these questions honestly and openly.

Use your journal to answer the following questions:

1. Would you say you are a "control freak?" Why or why not?

2. Make a list of things you feel are out of your control right now.

3. What would you change about your life if you could?

4. Do you think it is harder to trust God when life is hard? Explain in your journal.

5. What are you praying for most right now in your life?

6. Write about a time when God answered a prayer in your life.

7. Even if the worst thing possible happens in your life, do you think you can still trust God? Why or why not?

I am a planner. I like to set goals. There have been times in my life when I struggled with releasing control to God. One truth that helped me see things more clearly was this: I did not create myself; God created me, and He did so with a purpose in mind. If you like being in control of things in your life, maybe it will help you to stop and think about this truth. You had nothing to do with your existence. I know it sounds simple, but it is a good thought to ponder. You did not choose when you would be born. You did not choose your parents, your skin color, your height or your eye color. God created you. You were His idea! He chose your parents, your skin color, your height, your eye color and everything else. He gifted you in special ways to be used for His Kingdom. He had a purpose in mind when He formed you in your mother's womb. Look at the verse below as God is encouraging Jeremiah:

> *"Before I formed you in the womb I knew you, before*
> *you were born I set you apart; I appointed you as a*
> *prophet to the nations."*
> ~*Jeremiah 1:5*

You did not ask to be born. It was God who gave you life. He is the potter, and you are the clay. Isn't it interesting that the clay has one main job....to surrender to the potter? That is true for you and me, too! Our main job is to surrender to God.

SURRENDER
How do you define the word, surrender?

_____

_____

_____

_____

Surrender is an important word. It means to yield to the power, control, or possession of another. Surrendering to God means yielding your life over completely to Him. It sounds easy, but it can be difficult to surrender, especially when life takes an unexpected bad turn. When life is going along smoothly, it is easy to yield to God's plan, but when life is difficult and bad things happen, it is much harder to surrender to His plan. Believing God is in control over all things and yielding to Him is a lesson I began to learn the day I almost died.

I wonder if you know what day of the week Nov 20th was on in 2005. I do. It was a Sunday. The Sunday before Thanksgiving. It was almost my last day on Earth.

It's funny the things we don't know. I am a pharmacist. I am a healthcare provider, and I did not know that in America you could die from a stomach bug. Well, I'm here to tell you that you can. You can absolutely die from a stomach bug when you live in a first-world country...I almost did.

On November 20, 2005, I was 31 years old. Bryan and I had been married for over eight years. We were living in our new home. Our daughter Ellie was three years old, and our son Sam was nine months old. Our lives were full! I had just left my job as a practicing pharmacist to go teach at a university because God called me to teach. It was a significant pay cut for me to leave my community pharmacist job. I also went from only working four days a week to working five days a week at the university. I left a job seven minutes from home to now drive over 30 minutes to the university, all because God called me. I trusted Him and surrendered to what I felt was His call on my life. I could have never predicted what would happen a few short months into this new teaching position.

On the morning of November 20th, 2005, we went to church and then out to lunch with family. When we got home from lunch, I felt unusually tired, so I went to lie down. Bryan was watching a basketball game while Ellie played, and Sam took a nap. Later that afternoon, symptoms of a violent stomach virus started. I had not had a stomach bug since I was in high school. It came on me with a vengeance because it hit me very fast and hard!

I was extremely sick for several hours and I found myself completely lethargic, lying on the bathroom floor. I could barely move. I managed to pull myself up and look in the mirror. What I saw in the mirror scared me. I looked gray. Based on how I felt and how I looked, I knew I was in trouble. Bryan had no idea how fast things had progressed or how seriously ill I was. He assumed I was sleeping. I did not have the strength to call loudly enough for him to hear me, so I crawled to my bed and thought I would just sleep it off. As I started to drift off, I felt God urge me not to go to sleep.

About that time, Bryan came in to check on me. He panicked when he saw me! I had never been this sick before. He called my mom to come over and stay with our kids so he could drive me to the emergency room. In the car, I was very dizzy, and things were blurry.

By the time we arrived at the hospital, my kidneys were shutting down. My pulse was around 170 beats per minute and my blood pressure was 65/39 (normal is 120/80). The doctors told Bryan to let my family know the seriousness of what was happening. They also told Bryan if I would have tried to "sleep it off," I would have died.

A whole team of doctors and nurses came over to start working on me. Over the next few hours, they gave me eight liters of fluid in order to make my kidneys start working again. I was given multiple antibiotics and was monitored very closely for the next several days. After a short stay in the hospital, my body began to improve, but I was not out of the woods yet.

I improved and I came home from the hospital, but over the next six months, I struggled with more sickness and dehydration. I continued to have virus-like symptoms and was in and out of the hospital receiving bags of fluid on a regular basis. My resting heart rate was between 115-130 bpm (normal resting is around 70 bpm), so my heart was working as if I was always running a marathon. This made me lose significant weight.

I weighed 100 pounds even though I forced myself to eat. Everything went straight through me. This sent me mentally into a dark place. For the first time in my life, I had a health issue that was completely out of my control.

No matter how hard I tried, I could not get back to normal. I had no energy...none! And the worst part was no medical doctor could tell me what was wrong. No one could explain why I was so sick. None of this made sense and I wondered if I would ever get better. I would lie in my bed and ask God what He was trying to teach me. This was not a part of my plan.

While I was home alone throughout the day, I would say out loud to God, "Please let me learn whatever lesson I need to learn so I can get back to my life!" I begged Him to fix it. I begged Him to fix me. I went through anxiety and bouts of depression like I had never experienced before. I wondered if God heard my cries. I wondered if He cared. I wondered if this would be my new life.

Throughout this time, even though I had a loving husband and family, my mind went to scary places. I had fears my body would never recover, and I thought I might die. I wondered if I would be able to do the things I wanted to do in life. I worried about the medical bills and being out of work. I was stuck in the Cycle of Worry and I could not break free.

When I look back on this time in my life, I still remember how desperate I felt. I have vivid memories of me lying on the couch crying out to God and feeling like He did not see me. This season of life was hard, but if I had the chance to go back and change it (to where I never had the stomach virus), I would not change it. Through that valley of life, God taught me some of the most valuable lessons I have ever learned. The first being that I am not in control. He is in control over all things. I do not want you to misunderstand what that means. I am not saying we are robots on Earth programmed by God to only do what He wills. God gave us the gift of free will. We have the freedom to choose. We can choose what to eat, what kind of car to drive, etc.

Do you know what else we can choose? We can choose to surrender our lives to God, or not. God desires for us to choose Him, but He does not force us to choose Him. He does not make us use our giftedness for His glory. Although He loves us so much, He does not force us to love Him back.

The scripture in Jeremiah is such a perfect example of how God desires for us to yield to Him. We are not the potter in our lives. We are not God. When we try to be the ones in control, we limit ourselves from reaching the fullness of who God created us to be. It is only when we give ourselves fully to Him that we can be shaped and reshaped into a beautiful vessel.

During my illness, I felt very alone. I can look back now and see that God was with me, but during that time, I wasn't sure. My faith had come face-to-face with my fears. The darkness that surrounded me had clouded my faith. My feelings of fear and anxiety were bigger than my faith.

I did not want to be sick. I wanted to press the rewind button and go back to living my normal life. I wanted to go, and do, and be who I had always been. These fearful thoughts rolled around inside my head: "What if I never get better? What if I never have the energy I need to take care of my kids? What if this is my new life?" You see, I wanted to skip over this dark part of my life and get back to the way things were, but there was no skipping over it. The only way out of this darkness was to walk through it, and there was no guarantee I would ever feel normal again. God doesn't promise us an easy life, but He does promise us love, peace, and joy when we put our trust completely in Him.

There was no medical provider who could help me become healthy again. Life consisted of exhaustion, lack of sleep, losing weight, multiple bouts of diarrhea every day, the inability to work like I once did, and having an anxious spirit that was stealing my joy. That was my reality, and I had an important decision to make...how was I going to respond? You see, with all of the things that were out of my control, I still had control of how I chose to respond in this bad situation.

- What if I did not get better - did that mean God was not faithful? Did that mean I could not trust Him? Do I only trust Him when life is going smoothly? Can I trust Him when life is hard and confusing?

- What if I never had my same energy level again - did that mean I could not be a good mom? Did that mean I would choose to live with no joy or happiness?

- What if suffering from poor health would be my new reality - did that mean my life was not worth living? Did that mean I had been forgotten by God? Did that mean I would be mad at Him and blame Him until the day I die?

These are tough questions but they are real questions we often ask privately when something really bad happens to us.

You may have experienced a tragedy in your life that left you feeling like the darkness would never end. You may have experienced something that changed your life forever. If so, I am so sorry that happened to you. I am so sorry you experienced a darkness over your life that made you feel suffocated. I am so sorry you went through a painful experience that left you questioning the goodness of God.

My friend, as you have walked through trials and painful circumstances, I hope you know God is good in spite of those circumstances. He really is good and He loves you. I also hope you know you can trust in Him even when terrible things happen. You can trust in Him at your worst. You can trust in Him when life feels like it is falling apart.

I can't explain why bad things happen, and oh, how I wish there was a rewind button so we could go back and undo them. I don't need to tell you there is no rewind button. We both know there is no time machine. We cannot go back...but we can choose to keep living. We can choose to keep seeking after God. We can choose to keep chasing after joy! It is possible to choose joy even in the midst of the worst pain imaginable. We choose joy by choosing to walk closely with Jesus, and as we move forward one step at a time, we can choose to believe God is who He says He is. His promises are true!

As I was at home trying to recover from my illness, I read my Bible and prayed. I began to see I had an issue with control. You see, I wanted things *my* way. I wanted comfort, health, wealth, happiness, and all of the good things we think make for a successful life. God revealed to me that my desire to have such an easy life was preventing me from growing into the person He wanted me to be. I did not want discomfort, sickness, pain, or suffering. Who does? But what

I learned laying on my couch during that illness was invaluable to my walk with God. My faith was tested, and I learned to trust in Him in a way like never before.

There are certain lessons in life we can only learn in the uncertainties of life. Our faith must meet our darkest place because that is where our faith will be tested. You may have heard this saying before - a faith that is not tested is a faith that cannot be trusted. I believe that is true. Without trials and tests, our faith cannot grow. It cannot become strong. It cannot become complete.

My brethren, count it all joy when you fall into various trials, knowing that the testing of your faith produces patience. But let patience have its perfect work, that you may be perfect and complete, lacking nothing.
~James 1:2-4

Do we only believe in the hope of Jesus and the truths of God's Word when life is easy and comfortable? Or...do we also believe in the hope of Jesus and the truths of God's Word in our darkest hour? When a dark cloud of worry, uncertainty, and fear surrounds us, will we choose to stand on the Word of God? Will we choose to believe God's promises when life hurts? That choice leads us back to peace and joy.

During my illness, as the weeks and months went by, my body slowly recovered. I went back to work. I was able to be a wife and mom and live life again, but I was not the same person I was before November 20, 2005. Throughout that ordeal, I realized walking with God in full surrender meant I trusted the sovereignty of God. It meant I looked for His providence. I learned that surrendering to God did not mean

I should stop praying and asking God to move on my behalf. It did not mean I should stop petitioning Him for what my heart desired, but it did mean I needed to remember I am not in control of my life. God is in control over my life. He is God and I am not. He is the potter and I am the clay. My job is to die to myself and surrender fully to His will.

In the Garden of Gethsemane, before going to the cross, Jesus surrendered to His Father. Jesus is fully God and fully man. On Earth, Jesus felt the same things we feel. He felt many different emotions. The night before His crucifixion, we see a picture of His humanity. He was in anguish. He said this to His disciples:

"My soul is overwhelmed with sorrow to the point of death.
Stay here and keep watch with me." Going a little farther,
he fell with his face to the ground and prayed, "My Father,
if it is possible, may this cup be taken from me.
Yet not as I will, but as you will."
~Matthew 26:38-39

Jesus asked the Father, if it was possible, to let the cup be taken from Him. He asked God if there could be any other way to accomplish His will...to let it be. But, Jesus finished His prayer by yielding to the will of His Father as He prayed, "Yet not as I will, but as you will."

I love this picture of Jesus fully surrendering to the will of the Father. He yielded his will over to the Father. We, too, need to yield our will over to the Father. Releasing control means we surrender everything to God. Everything. It's only when we give ourselves over to Him fully that we can become the vessel He desires us to become.

The question is....are we moldable? Are we willing to give complete control over to Him to do whatever He desires in our lives?

My friend, God wants us to be moldable. He wants us to be clay in His hands. He wants us to put our trust in Him completely. He wants us to give our lives over to Him. Will we give complete control to Him? Will we choose to trust in Him even when something terrible happens to us that changes our lives forever? Will we put our trust in Him even when we do not understand? Will we put our trust in Him even when we are scared and uncertain?

With our arms stretched out are we brave enough to say to the potter with an honest and vulnerable heart - "I want Your will, God. Whatever, however, whenever, wherever. I surrender to You."? You can trust God with your life...your whole life. Below are a few suggestions on what to do next:

- Get alone with God and pray. Ask Him to reveal to you the areas of your life where you are holding onto control. What have you been unable to release to Him?
- Write those things down. Come face to face with them so you can be aware of what to pray for.
- Ask God to help you give control over to Him. It may not happen overnight, but you can begin the process right now.

You can use the sentences below as you begin to pray:

"You are God, and I am not. I struggle with having control, Lord. Today, I give You my whole life, not just parts of it. As much as I know how I want to give You control. I am choosing to trust You with everything in my life and the lives of the people I love. You are the potter and I am the clay. I give You control over..."

_____

_____

_____

_____

_____

_____

_____

_____

_____

_____

_____

_____

_____

_____

_____

_____

_____

_____

_____

 Releasing control means you choose to trust God with the outcome.

A white flag is often used as a symbol of surrender. Write on the flag below what (or who) you need to surrender over to God. Maybe you are worried about your health. Maybe it's a relationship you are worried about. Whatever it is, write it on the flag and pray diligently for God to help you trust Him with it.

A Prescription for Joy
STEP FOUR

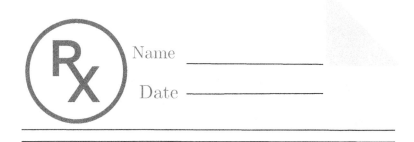

Name _____

Date _____

Pray and ask God to help you give control
over to Him
Memorize Isaiah 64:8
Memorize Proverbs 16:9
Choose to surrender your plans to God

_____   Dr. Joy
Date   Signature

124

A prayer for releasing control

Lord, You are the potter and I am the clay. This means I can choose to put my trust in You! You promise that as I surrender to You, You will help me and You will direct my steps. I need You, God. I need You to help me release control of my life to You! I need You to help me release my struggles with worry to You. I know You have a good plan for my life and I want to live inside Your plan. Thank You, Lord, for loving me. Thank You for helping me. Amen.

Trust in the Lord with all your heart, and do not lean on your own understanding. In all your ways acknowledge him, and he will make straight your paths.
~Proverbs 3:5-6

Thoughts from Step Four

Take a few minutes to write down what encouraged you from this section. What main points do you want to remember and use in your life?

_____

_____

_____

_____

_____

_____

_____

_____

_____

_____

_____

_____

_____

_____

_____

_____

_____

_____

_____

_____

Step Five

YOUR HOPE
IS IN JESUS

FAITH AND TRUST

Step Five: Your Hope is in Jesus

Do you wear contact lenses or glasses? Did you know that about 75% of adults use some sort of vision correction? Maybe you are wearing reading glasses right now as you read this chapter. I am wearing my reading glasses as I am writing it.

I had excellent vision until I started college. Many of my college science classes were very large, with nearly 500 students. Early in the fall semester, I grabbed a seat toward the back of the class, but as the semester progressed, my ability to see the words on the screen diminished. They were blurry. After a visit to my optometrist, and a new pair of glasses on my face, the words on the screen became crystal clear.

Glasses help people see more clearly. Glasses work by bending light. This makes the light focus correctly on the retina. This produces a clear image and allows people to have better vision. Let's keep this in mind as we dive a little deeper into overcoming excessive worry.

THE RIGHT PERSPECTIVE

What is your perspective when bad things happen? What does it do to your faith? Let me clarify this question a little more.

When bad things happen in life, we often become fearful, and we know that worry is rooted in fear. The enemy uses worry as a weapon against us to keep our hearts far from Jesus. He uses worry to tempt us to doubt the goodness of

God. He uses worry to tempt us to doubt the faithfulness of God. When bad things happen, we can be tempted to question God and even our purpose in life.

Worry steals our hope.

When life is hard, and things do not make sense, we can start looking at life through the blurry lens of worry. It overtakes our perspective and leads us down a path of uncertainty. As we seek to overcome worry, what we need is a new perspective. Just like using a new pair of glasses helps our eyes focus more clearly on the world around us, when worry creeps into our lives, we need to refocus our minds on truth. We need a better, crystal-clear view of God through the lens of His Word.

Viewing the world from the lens of God's Word clears up our blurry interpretation of the chaos going on around us. Viewing the world from the lens of God's Word helps us see that He never loses control over all things, and His plan is always good.

For we are his workmanship, created in Christ Jesus
for good works, which God prepared beforehand,
that we should walk in them.
~Ephesians 2:10

We know we should keep our focus on Jesus, but the real question is, "How do we do that when life falls apart?" Often, we know *what* we need to do, but we do not always know *how*. How do we refocus our perspective when bad things happen? We begin by examining what we believe about God. Faith is the starting point, and God's Word says faith comes by hearing the Word of God.

So then faith comes by hearing, and
hearing by the word of God.
~Romans 10:17

You and I have a big decision to make about the Bible. If we believe the Bible is true, then we have what we need to stand firm on what the Bible says. Believing God's Word as truth enables us to live our lives with confidence because we know God's promises are true. This helps us see things more clearly. We can live with joyful hope and rely on Him when life is hard.

All Scripture is God-breathed and is useful for teaching,
rebuking, correcting and training in righteousness,
so that the servant of God may be thoroughly
equipped for every good work.
~2 Timothy 3:16-17

In the space below, write down any struggles you have believing the Bible is the truth of God's Word.

_____

_____

_____

_____

I came to know Jesus at a young age. I received Him as my Lord and Savior at the age of nine, but there was so much I did not understand. As I grew older, I'm sad to admit my knowledge of God's Word did not grow along with me. I did not plug into discipleship opportunities. I did not spend dedicated time reading my Bible. I hung my faith on my belief that Jesus was the Son of God, He died on a cross to save me from hell, and He rose from the grave on the third day.

Although these truths are the foundation of the Christian faith, there is more we can do to know God intimately. Jesus wants us to have childlike faith, but as we grow and mature physically, we should grow and mature spiritually as well.

As a result, we are no longer to be children, tossed here
and there by waves and carried about by every wind
of doctrine, by the trickery of people, by craftiness
in deceitful scheming; but speaking the truth in love,
we are to grow up in all aspects into Him who is
the head, that is Christ.
~Ephesians 4:14-15

What I did not realize was although my personal relationship with Jesus should be the most important thing in my life, I would never fully know the will of God unless I knew the Word of God. I would never have the right perspective on life unless I studied the Bible.

As you examine your heart and mind regarding what you believe about God, I wonder if you have unanswered questions about Him? I think most of us do. There are some questions we do not have answers for.

As followers of Jesus, we walk by faith, not by sight, but I've also learned that walking by faith does not give me an excuse to ignore the importance of understanding God's Word. The more I study the Bible, the more I learn who God is. I learn about His heart and His character. The more I seek to know God, the more wisdom He gives me. The more I seek to know Him, the better I discern His will. Worry can cause us to feel hopeless. Satan wants us to stay away from our Bibles because he knows we will find the hope we are looking for in the pages of God's Word.

When I was in my late 20s, my pastor's wife facilitated a video-based women's Bible study. At that time in my faith journey, I did not spend a lot of time reading my Bible. I had not grown very much in my walk with the Lord. There were parts of the Bible that intimidated me. There were parts of the Bible I had trouble understanding.

When I learned about this new Bible study being offered at my church, I decided to attend. I did not have high expectations for the study but I wanted to give it a try. As our group watched the first session, I was amazed at what I learned. The Bible teacher in the video explained things so clearly. It helped me better understand the context of the scripture. I remember thinking, "Wow! I wish I understood the Bible that way."

Each week, as our group dove deeper into God's Word through that study, a spark began to ignite inside my heart. I felt God tugging at my heart. I felt convicted. I realized I was missing out on so many beautiful details about who God is because I had not dedicated my time or energy to reading and studying the Bible.

At that time in my life, I was teaching a small college Sunday School class at my church. I only had seven college students who participated and that was on a good Sunday. Sometimes no one would show up. Each week, I usually looked over the lesson the Saturday night before I would teach. I did not put my heart or energy into this class. Over the course of the video-based Bible study, God convicted my heart about the small amount of time I was spending each week preparing to teach my college Sunday School class. I began to feel guilty that I was not putting in the needed effort. I felt the Holy Spirit convict me about this truth: I will make time for what is important to me.

God brought to my mind how much I studied when I was in college. Back then, I made time to study because I wanted to do well in my classes. It was important to me. I wanted to become a pharmacist and I knew it would require hard work and dedication. In college, I had a detailed plan on how much time I would spend each day studying for my exams and projects. I put my heart into my work because it mattered to me.

It's a hard truth to swallow, but I believe it is true - we will make time for what really matters to us. Being a part of this Bible Study caused me to ask myself this question: why was knowing God not that important to me? Why did I only spend a short amount of time reading my Bible each week? Why did I not put my heart into teaching my college Sunday School class?

God used this Bible study to help transform my perspective. Not only did God use it to reveal Himself to me more, but He also used it to show me where I fell short. I needed to change my habits. I was missing out on knowing Him more because I was not putting my heart into reading His Word. I was missing out on finding real hope and joy in my life because I did not know God's Word very well. One evening on my way home from Bible Study, I was alone in my car. I felt convicted about how little time I spent reading my Bible. I prayed a simple prayer that went something like this:

"God, I want to know You more. I am sorry I have not spent more time in Your Word. I confess to You that I have not loved Your Word the way I should. Will You help me? Will You give me a love for Your Word, and will You open my heart and my mind to understand it more?"

I prayed this prayer from a sincere heart. This Bible study sparked a fire inside of me that caused me to want to be different. I wanted to know God more, but that did not mean God would automatically infuse more knowledge of His Word into my brain. In order for me to know God more, I had to be a person of action. I had to DO something different than what I had been doing. It was not enough to simply have a desire or a wish for my faith to grow. If I wanted to experience God on a deeper level, I needed to put in more effort and energy. I needed to spend time in His Word and I needed to obey His Word. Hearing and reading the Word of God leads to greater faith. Loving and obeying God leads to knowing Him more.

Whoever has my commands and keeps them is the one who loves me. The one who loves me will be loved by my Father, and I too will love them and show myself to them.
~John 14:21

But He said, "On the contrary, blessed are those who hear the word of God and observe it."
~Luke 11:28

I have hidden your word in my heart that I might not sin against you.
~Psalm 119:11

If I wanted to understand the Bible better, I needed a plan of action and an obedient heart. I needed to make changes in my life. Now, let's take a quick pause as I want to share with you some tips that helped me study the Bible. You may already have a great strategy for how you read and study the Bible. If so, that is awesome! But, if you struggle with reading the Bible and understanding it, maybe my journey will be helpful. I would like to share a few study methods I use.

As I thought about how I could grow my faith, I thought about the study strategies I used when I was in pharmacy school. Back then, I would find a quiet place where I could spread out all of my materials. I would open my notes from class and my textbook. I had highlighters, a legal pad, and some caffeine. There was so much material to learn and I needed to digest it in small sections. As I read my notes from class, I wrote down the most important points on a separate sheet of paper. I used colorful highlighters to help the material stick in my mind. I decided to try this same study strategy to study the Bible.

In my journey to know God's Word more, I started by buying a new study Bible. I bought a set of Bible highlighters and some notepads. Since I was already teaching a Sunday School class at my church, that is where I decided to start...with the Sunday School Teacher's Guide. Each week, instead of studying the lesson on Saturday night, I started reading the lesson earlier in the week. As I read the lesson, I took notes on a separate sheet of paper. I read the corresponding scripture in my study Bible and I looked up the scripture passage online to see what Bible scholars had to say. I wrote down the most important takeaways from the passage and I highlighted the important points I wanted to stick in my mind.

It felt so good to dive deeper into the scripture, and when I came to church each Sunday, I had more confidence in my knowledge of God's Word. The more I studied and prepared, the better I felt about the important responsibility I had to teach my class. As I poured over God's Word to prepare to teach each week, God's Word poured into me.

Do your best to present yourself to God as one approved,
a worker who does not need to be ashamed and who
correctly handles the word of truth.
~2 Timothy 2:15

Not many of you should become teachers, my fellow
believers, because you know that we who teach will
be judged more strictly.
~James 3:1

As I made this a habit in my life, over the years, I began to understand God's Word on a deeper level and do you know what happened? I began to love His Word. God answered that prayer I prayed years ago and He gave me a love for His Word. He used a women's Bible Study to show me I needed to make changes in my life. My perspective on how I approached God's Word shifted, and my faith grew.

I wonder if you ever struggle with understanding the Bible. If so, I understand how you feel. It can be difficult to know where to start and what to do. I am encouraged by knowing God is not a God of confusion. He is not a "hide-and-seek" God who wants to stay hidden from us. God does not just want us to know about Him, He wants us to know Him, and to experience Him, personally!

As you and I take steps to know Him more, He promises to meet us right where we are.

Draw near to God and He will draw near to you.
~James 4:8

If you have the desire to spend more time in God's Word, I hope you will find just the right study strategy that works well for you. Setting aside study time later in the evenings is what worked for me, but you may be more of a morning person. No matter how you make it work, God will meet you there as you make more time for Him.

If you are not sure where to start, I encourage you to start right where you are. Plug into a Bible study at your church or find one online. Pray and ask God to show you where to plug in. You can be sure He will guide you to where you need to be.

God wants you to grow in a deeper knowledge of Him. If you want to understand the Bible more, take a few minutes to think about the questions below:

- What Biblical resources do you have?
- What Biblical resources do you need?
- What time of day can you set aside to read and study?
- What steps can you take to stick with your plan?

As for God, his way is perfect:
The Lord's word is flawless;
he shields all who take refuge in him.
~Psalm 18:30

I hope you are encouraged to know God more! I hope you feel inspired to make a plan to study His Word and stick with it! You can be open and honest with your questions about God. As you seek to know more and dig in on a deeper level, you can settle those questions in your heart and mind. Sometimes what we need most is a new perspective on life. As we grow in our knowledge of who God is, our life's focus becomes clearer.

I'm excited to see how He speaks into your heart and life as you continue to fight back against worry. As worry tries to blur your vision by stealing your hope and joy, remember Jesus came to give you hope and joy! His hope and joy can be found within the pages of your Bible.

Step five in overcoming excessive worry is understanding the true meaning of hope. My hope and your hope are in Jesus, and when I think about the hope of Jesus, I think about the promise of Heaven. We read about Heaven in scripture, but can you imagine what it will look like? Can you imagine what it will be like? I want to tell you about a dream I had years ago about Heaven. It was a dream that made a lasting impact on my life.

Have you ever wondered where dreams come from? This has been an age-old question that many people have contemplated. Some dreams make no sense, like the ones where you are falling, being chased, or you find yourself back in school taking a big test that you did not prepare for. Those are the three most common dreams according to experts. Isn't it interesting that all three of these dreams are centered around anxious situations?

On occasion, we have a dream that makes a lasting impact on our lives. These dreams often cause us to wake up a hot mess and we have trouble going back to sleep afterwards. Have you ever had a dream where you felt like God was trying to tell you something? That's the kind of dream I had not long after my mother-in-law passed away. I dreamed I went to Heaven and it was a dream I will never forget. I want to share part of my dream with you.

I dreamed I was in a car accident, and as my car began rolling down the embankment, my soul flew out of my body and went into the arms of an angel. The angel had tall, beautiful wings and I was in awe of his beauty. As I sat cradled in his arms, I watched as my car rolled down the embankment. The angel took me to what I believed at the time was Heaven. I heard beautiful music playing and I saw people dressed in beautiful clothes fellowshipping with one another. They were laughing and smiling and enjoying each other's company.

My mother-in-law came to greet me, and I still remember the happiness that flowed out of my heart when I saw her! I cried tears of joy as we hugged. I did not want to let her go. She grabbed my hand and pulled me away from the crowd and we walked through the lush green grass over to a white table.

As we sat down, I could not take my eyes off of her. She looked just like I remembered her before she was sick, only a younger, more beautiful version. I tried to remain calm as we began talking, but my heart was about to burst with excitement. I had a million questions I wanted to ask her. As I started asking my questions, she graciously answered each one until I asked my last question.

I asked her what God looked like.

She looked at me with her bright blue eyes and shook

her head from side to side as if to say she could not answer that question. At that moment, I was suddenly back in the arms of the beautiful angel. As I sat cradled in his arms, I looked down to see the bottom of the embankment where my damaged car laid upside down. He whispered to me that my time with him was up. I begged him not to send me back. I pleaded with him, and as I held onto him with all my strength, I heard a loud sound. It sounded like a rushing wind. He tossed my soul back toward my body, and I abruptly woke up.

I was in my bed at home with Bryan who was sleeping peacefully beside me. My heart was racing. I was wet with sweat. I felt overwhelmed but encouraged all at the same time. This dream was not the kind of dream you can just go back to sleep from. To me, this dream felt more than just a dream. It felt like God had given me a tiny glimpse of Heaven.

We know from God's Word that He speaks to people in dreams, but does He still speak that way? God is God. He can do anything He chooses to do. I do not know if my dream was God revealing a piece of Heaven to me or not, but I do know how I felt when I woke up. I had more hope about Heaven than I had before I went to bed that night. I had an excitement in my heart that affirmed the promises of God. God's Word tells us that Heaven is real and when we belong to Jesus, we will go there and be with Him forever!

The wall was made of jasper, and the city of pure gold,
as pure as glass. The foundations of the city walls
were decorated with every kind of precious stone.
The first foundation was jasper, the second sapphire,
the third agate, the fourth emerald, the fifth onyx,

the sixth ruby, the seventh chrysolite, the eighth beryl, the ninth topaz, the tenth turquoise, the eleventh jacinth, and the twelfth amethyst. The twelve gates were twelve pearls, each gate made of a single pearl. The great street of the city was of gold, as pure as transparent glass.
~Revelation 18:18-21

The brilliance of Heaven makes my heart long for Heaven. What a place it must be - and what joy we will experience as we will be with God forever.

In this section, we have been working through our thoughts about who God is and what we believe about the Bible. We are working on our perspective. What you and I believe about God and His Word is critical to our perspective on life and our success in overcoming worry. The Bible is not merely a book of good advice or practical living. It is not merely a book of exciting stories and miracles. The Bible is about Jesus. It is His story. From beginning to end, the Bible tells the incredible story of how God became a man in order to rescue mankind. From Genesis to Revelation, the Bible is a story of redemption. It is a story of love. It is a story of hope. It is through the pages of our Bibles that we learn about eternity. We read about Heaven. We learn that Heaven is a place with no more pain or sadness. There will be no darkness and no sadness. It will be the most beautiful place; so beautiful it is impossible for us to imagine how magnificent it will be.

It is through the pages of our Bibles that God reveals His Son, Jesus to us. The Bible is all about His story to rescue the world from sin. In the last chapter, I asked you to think about the question, "Who is Jesus?" This question is the most important "life question" you and I will ever answer. Jesus asked His disciples a similar question.

When Jesus came to the region of Caesarea Philippi,
he asked his disciples, "Who do people say the Son of
Man is?""They replied, "Some say John the Baptist; others
say Elijah; and still others, Jeremiah or one of the prophets."
"But what about you?" he asked. "Who
do you say I am?" Simon Peter answered, "You
are the Messiah, the Son of the living God."
~Matthew 16:13-16

You may be wondering what answering this question has to do with overcoming worry. Well, friend, it has everything to do with overcoming worry because one of the greatest tools God has given us to overcome worry is the gift of hope!

The English word, "hope" is typically defined as "wanting something to happen or be the case." We say things like, "I hope I can go to the beach this weekend, or I hope I win the race." Our English use of the word hope is often synonymous with wishful thinking. We have a desire for something to happen in our lives. Our use of the word hope does not always mean we expect something to happen.

When we see the word "hope" used in the Bible, it has a much stronger meaning. The Greek word in the Bible used for hope is "elpis." It means "desiring something good with an expectation of obtaining it." Did you notice the word, expectation? Biblical hope is more than just wishful thinking. It is more than wondering if something may or may not happen. Biblical hope is *expecting* hope and it is centered around what we know is to come. It is centered around confidence. It is centered on certainty. This type of hope is who Jesus is. Jesus is the hope of the world, and as we walk our life's journey, we can walk it with expectation, confidence, and certainty. Not because of who we are, and not because of what gifts we bring to the table, but because of who Jesus is and the salvation He brings to the world.

And his name will be the hope of all the world.
~Matthew 12:21

Real hope is found in a person and His name is Jesus.

We wait in hope for the Lord;
he is our help and our shield.
~Psalm 33:20

Until we understand that Jesus came to rescue us from sin, pay the price for our sins, and save us from our sins by laying down His life, we will never have real hope. Without real hope, we will never have real joy and peace. Without joy and peace, we will never overcome worry.

"May the God of hope fill you with all joy and peace."
~Romans 15:13

As we look at changing our perspective on worry, hope is the lens we need to clear up our blurry vision.

I pray that the eyes of your heart may be enlightened in order
that you may know the hope to which he has called you, the
riches of his glorious inheritance in his holy people.
~Ephesians 1:18

We live in a fallen world. Our world is full of heartache, disappointment, pain, and regret. If we only focus our eyes on what we see in this world, we will have hearts full of fear, worry, stress, anxiety, depression, and disappointment. The good news is because of Jesus, this earthly world is not our home. It is not our final destination. As followers of Jesus, we can take off our earthly lens and put on our heavenly lens. Our eyes can look ahead and envision what is to come. Our eyes can look ahead to Heaven. We cannot see it fully on this side of eternity, but because of Jesus, one day we will see and experience eternity with Him.

So we fix our eyes not on what is seen, but on what is unseen, since what is seen is temporary, but what is unseen is eternal.
~2 Corinthians 4:18

Putting on our lens of hope helps us see more clearly, but what about when bad things happen in our lives? Those bad things often spark fear in our hearts and that can lead to worry. My friend, it is important for us to remember that following Jesus is not all rainbows and sunshine.

There is suffering that comes with following Jesus. Suffering is not a warm and fuzzy word. Most of us do not want to suffer. In fact, our prayers are usually against suffering. We ask God to take away the things that make us feel uncomfortable. We ask Him to remove the pain.

When I think about my own prayer life, I often pray for comfort. I often pray for what is easy for me. Most of us prefer the mountaintop experience instead of being in the valleys of life, but it is difficult for us to grow spiritually when we only have mountaintop experiences. In my own faith journey, some of my greatest spiritual growth happened in the middle of my suffering. It happened in the valley.

Jesus never promised an easy life. He told us it would be hard. As His followers, we lay down our lives to follow Him.

Then Jesus said to his disciples, "Whoever wants to be my disciple must deny themselves and take up their cross and follow me."
~Matthew 16:24

Laying down our old lives and worldly comforts can be difficult because it takes a fully surrendered heart and a life that is willing to sacrifice. When we give our lives over to Jesus, and then God allows us to go through suffering, it can be scary and confusing. We sometimes believe the lie that if we live our lives obeying God then nothing bad will happen. Surely God will give me an easy and comfortable life if I live for Him. But, that is not what the Bible says. The Bible says we will face trials of many kinds. This means we will face times of pain and suffering.

Describe a time when you went through suffering? How did it affect your faith?

_____

_____

_____

_____

_____

_____

_____

_____

In my life, when I experienced times of suffering, God grew my faith in Him. He reminded me that my suffering is not in vain. It is through my suffering that I realize my need for God. It is through my pain that I realize my dependence on Him. It is through my heartache that I yearn for closeness with God. Although I may not understand why God allows me to experience pain and suffering, I am confident He has a purpose for it.

There is purpose in your pain and suffering, and Jesus promises to work it for good.

The Lord will fulfill his purpose for me;
your steadfast love, O Lord, endures forever.
Do not forsake the work of your hands.
~Psalm 138:8

What pain have you experienced recently in your life? Do you believe you can find peace in the middle of heartache and pain? Explain in the space below:

_____

_____

_____

_____

_____

_____

_____

_____

When you go through suffering and pain, you can still have peace in your spirit. You find His peace by standing firm on what you know is true from God's Word. You find His peace by knowing His promises are true and you can cling to those promises.

There is a sense of comfort I have found in the midst of pain and suffering. When I remember this life is only temporary, it makes the pain and suffering more bearable. The trials of this life will not last forever. Because of Jesus, in the middle of my pain and suffering, I have hope. I am confident He has a purpose for my trial and I am sure there are better days ahead.

My friend, I do not know what you have been through or what you are going through right now in your life. You may be enduring burdens in your life that feel unbearable. I want you to remember because of Jesus, you have hope! His promises are true - He is with you. He is for you. He will never leave you. Through Him, you can find the hope you need to keep going even when life feels like it is falling apart.

Do not give up and do not quit. Remember, the painful burdens you endure will only last a little while. Because of Jesus, we have the promise of Heaven. He has gone to prepare a place for us and one day we will be with Him, forever!

My Father's house has many rooms; if that were not so, would
I have told you that I am going there to prepare a place for
you? And if I go and prepare a place for you, I will come back
and take you to be with me that you also may be where I am.
~John 14:2-3

My mother-in-law's name was Terry. She was wonderful. She was diagnosed with breast cancer at the age of 38. At the time of her diagnosis, I was 16 and Bryan was a senior in high school. Bryan's sister, Julie, was 15. Bryan and I had been dating for a little over a year when Terry found a large lump in her breast. Her doctors acted quickly and within weeks, she went in for surgery. All of this was happening during Bryan's senior year of high school. You know how busy, exciting, and scary that time of life is for a 17-year-old young man. He was making big decisions about his future while his mom was having surgery to remove her breast. It was a scary time for everyone.

After Terry's mastectomy, we learned that her cancer had progressed too far for standard care. Out of 30+ lymph nodes removed, 23 tested positive for cancer. She was given a 5% chance of survival. She and Bill would move to Vanderbilt Hospital, hours away in Tennessee, so Terry could undergo experimental chemotherapy through a clinical trial. She would be there for months.

The day after Bryan's high school graduation, Bryan's mom and dad left for Tennessee. We did not know if we would ever see Terry again. Experimental chemotherapy is dangerous and, at that time, oncologists and scientists knew much less than they know today about cancer therapy. When Bryan's mom and dad pulled out of the driveway to head to Tennessee, we were clinging to God. We were clinging to faith. We were clinging to hope. We had hope that the experimental treatments would work. We had hope that Terry would come back home, healed. We had hope she would be given more years to live. It was hope that kept everyone's spirit alive.

What a blessing it was when we learned the clinical trial was a success. It was a miracle for our family! Terry's cancer went into remission and what a celebration we had when she finally came home months later!

We were given several more years with Terry before the cancer returned. We were heartbroken when it violently metastasized to her lung, liver, and bones and she was not given a good prognosis. That year, two days before Christmas, Terry was admitted to the hospice wing of a large hospital an hour from our home. Bryan and I had been married for seven months and Julie and her fiancé, Ron, were getting married the following February. We all took time away from work and school to be with Terry. During those weeks, I prayed with desperation and begged God to heal my mother-in-law. I even tried bargaining with God to give her just a few more months of life so she could be at Julie's wedding in February. I believed, I hoped, and I pleaded with God, but in the end, God did not choose to heal Terry on this side of eternity. Terry left this Earth for her heavenly home at the young age of 46. Julie married Ron exactly one month later. Terry was unable to be at her daughter's wedding.

Life is short. When we put life in its proper perspective, we do not have many years on this Earth. We do not understand why God chooses to grant some prayers but not others, but I've come to realize He does not owe us an explanation. He is God. When life turns upside down, what you and I need to cling to is the character of God. Life is full of ups and downs, but God does not change.

- When life is happy, God is good.
- When life is hard, God is still good.
- God is good all the time.

We can choose to trust in Him even when life doesn't make sense. Jesus told us we would have trouble in this world, but He also told us where our hope is found...in Him!

"I have told you these things, so that in me you may have peace. In this world you will have trouble. But take heart! I have overcome the world."
~John 16:33

Pain and suffering are a part of life. When we go through difficult times, our minds often fill up with fear, and we know that worry is rooted in fear. When worry creeps into your heart and mind, remember that your hope is not found in the things of this world. Your hope is not found in your finances. Your hope is not found in your spouse. Your hope is not found in your health. Your hope is not found in your education. Your hope is found in Jesus Christ, the one who left Heaven to come to Earth because He loves you! The one who died for you! The one who defeated death! Jesus is your hope!

God has a purpose for allowing pain in our lives, and one thing that helps us through the pain is knowing we have eternity in Heaven waiting for us. Our pain is covered with hope because when we belong to God, we have the assured hope of being with Him forever in our heavenly home.

Our purpose in life is not to live pain-free, stress-free, comfortable, lives. Our purpose in life is not to avoid suffering and heartache. Our purpose in life is to know Jesus, surrender our lives to Him, obey Him, love Him with all of who we are, and share His love with the world. He is the way, the truth, and the life. He is our life.

THE BLUE FLOWER

It was during those years of studying the Bible more intentionally that I felt a call on my life to begin a women's ministry. I did not feel qualified for this task, but I had a fire in my spirit to encourage women in their walk with God.

Over the next several years, our family moved to Jackson, Tennessee (10 hours from home) where God called me to begin Joytime Ministries. In preparing to start a nonprofit Christian ministry, I had a friend design the ministry logo with a red flower. Red represents the blood of Christ and red is my favorite color. I was only days away from publishing the Joytime logo with a red flower when Bryan and I attended our church's Sunday evening service. Our pastor spoke about the meaning of blue flowers. He shared about C.S. Lewis's autobiography, *Surprised by Joy* where Lewis references the blue flower when he speaks about his childhood.

Blue flowers are the rarest flowers found in the world and throughout history, they have been recognized as a symbol of longing and hope. As Bryan and I listened to the beautiful meaning of the blue flower, Bryan leaned over and whispered, "We need to change that red flower to blue." So we did!

God has set eternity inside the human heart. We have a longing in our hearts to leave the cares and stresses of this world for a better, perfect place. We long for a place with no more pain or suffering. We long for Heaven. We long to be with God. The blue flower in the Joytime logo is a symbol of what is to come but is unattainable right now...Heaven. The blue flower is a symbol of the assured hope we have of spending eternity with God!

He has made everything beautiful in its time. He has also
set eternity in the human heart; yet no one can fathom
what God has done from beginning to end.
~Ecclesiastes 3:11

When life feels overwhelming, keep your eyes on Jesus. He is your joy. He is your peace. He is your hope!

A Prescription for Joy
STEP FIVE

Name _____

Date _____

_____

Talk to God about any doubts you have in
your faith

Make a detailed plan on how you will study
God's Word

Memorize Romans 8:28

Find a Bible study to join

_____ Dr. Joy

Date   Signature

A prayer for
your hope is in Jesus

Thank You, God, that this life is not the end. This life is only the beginning. When we confess Jesus as Lord and Savior of our lives, our eternity is secured. When we put our trust in Him, we are made new. Thank You that we have real hope in Jesus. The pains and sufferings I experience on Earth are only temporary. Please help me when I face hard times in my life. Thank You for the promise and hope of Heaven that only comes through You! Amen.

But our citizenship is in heaven. And we eagerly await a Savior from there, the Lord Jesus Christ.
~Philippians 3:20

Thoughts from Step Five

Take a few minutes to write down what encouraged you from this section. What main points do you want to remember and use in your life?

_____

_____

_____

_____

_____

_____

_____

_____

_____

_____

_____

_____

_____

_____

_____

_____

_____

_____

_____

_____

_____

_____

Final Encouragement from Step Five:

Friend, in order for us to find real hope and joy, we must surrender our lives completely to Jesus. Salvation is found in Him, alone. We must believe in Him and then receive Him as Savior and Lord. When you search your heart, have you given your life fully to Jesus? Have you put your complete trust in Him? Is your eternity secured? Explain below:

_____

_____

_____

_____

_____

_____

_____

If you have any doubts about your salvation, please talk to a pastor of a Bible-believing church. Being saved is not simply walking down an aisle and being dunked in water through baptism. Salvation is understanding you are a sinner who needs a Savior, believing Jesus is the Son of God who came to Earth, lived a perfect life and died a criminal's death on a cross to pay the price for your sin. He defeated death and rose again on the third day. Being saved is yielding your life to Him completely and choosing to live for Him for the rest of your life. Jesus must not only be your Savior, He must also be your Lord.

Summary

PUTTING THE PIECES TOGETHER

MAKING IT STICK

Putting the Pieces Together

Overcoming excessive worry does not happen overnight. It takes work. It takes practice. It takes determination.

I know how worry can steal someone's life away. It tried to steal mine. I was sick and tired of how worry affected me and how it made me be someone I did not want to be. I was frustrated with how it caused me to lose sleep, feel nervous, have stomach issues, not eat and feel like a dark cloud surrounded me. I wanted my joyful life back. I wanted to be free from the chains of excessive worry.

Now that we have worked through the important steps needed to overcome worry, it is time to start using them in your life. It is time to kick worry to the curb. It is time to fight back!

When I was at my lowest point in life with worry, my initial response was to curl up in a ball in my bed and cry out to God. It felt like worry had me down for the count. I felt defeated and did not know how to fight back. I begged God to take the feeling away. I pleaded with Him to fix it. I wanted Him to make me feel normal again.

Through this difficult journey, I learned that God wants me to be strong and courageous. He wants me to know that through Jesus, I have exactly what I need to overcome my struggle with worry. Because of Him, I have hope. I have faith, and faith is being sure of what we hope for and certain of what we do not see (Hebrews 11:1).

When we read about heroes in the Bible whom God used to do miraculous things, we see them as people of action. They all had to DO something in order to experience victory.

When God parted the Red Sea, He did not tell the people to stand back and wait for the water to part on its own. He told

Moses to do something. As Moses held up his staff and stretched out his hand over the sea, the waters parted.

Raise your staff and stretch out your hand over the sea to divide the water so that the Israelites can go through the sea on dry ground.
~Exodus 14:16

When God parted the Jordan River and the Israelites walked into the promised land, the priests had to put their feet into the Jordan River before the waters parted.

And as soon as the priests who carry the ark of the LORD— the Lord of all the earth—set foot in the Jordan, its waters flowing downstream will be cut off and stand up in a heap.
~Joshua 3:13

In order for God to use Esther to save the annihilation of the Jewish people, Esther had to risk her life and go request a meeting with the King.

"And then I will go in to the king, which is not in accordance with the law; and if I perish, I perish."
~Esther 4:16b

Time and time again in God's Word, we see His people being required to go...to do...to act! Faith requires action in order to experience victory.

Many times in my life I wanted God to just fix whatever was wrong in my life. I wanted Him to magically make it go away. This is not the pattern of God we see throughout

His Word. He is not a magic genie waiting to give us three wishes. He is the holy, sovereign, mighty God who is growing His children to be more like His Son, Jesus. Even Jesus, who used mud to heal a blind man, sent that man to go and do something before he was able to see.

> *After saying this, he spit on the ground, made some mud*
> *with the saliva, and put it on the man's eyes. "Go,"*
> *he told him, "wash in the Pool of Siloam" (this*
> *word means "Sent"). So the man went and washed,*
> *and came home seeing.*
> *~John 9:6-7*

My friend, if you want to overcome the effects of excessive worry in your life, you will need to do something different than you are currently doing. Don't let that scare you. Instead, let that energize you! You can be a person of action!

I hope you are so sick and tired of being weighed down with worry that you are ready to put the five steps for overcoming worry into action. I want you to be so outdone by how worry is stealing your joy that you are ready to fight back.

It will take practice to form new habits, but it is worth the effort to overcome the effects of worry. Remember - worry is a tool Satan uses to steal your joy. He wants you to focus on all of the things that could go wrong in your life. He wants to shake your faith. Don't let him. Choose to listen to what God says about who you are and the good plan He has for you. Choose to know Him more. May your faith be bigger than your fear.

Be mindful of these steps and tools we have covered. Study them. Memorize them. Use them!

CONTROL YOUR INNER VOICE

Not every thought that comes into your mind should be allowed to stay there. Pay attention to what thoughts come into your mind. Kick out the ones that are damaging and take control of your thoughts.

CHANGE THE CHANNEL

When an anxious thought comes into your mind, you have control over what you do with it. Choose <u>not</u> to dwell on it. Instead, change the channel to stop thinking about that anxious thought and start thinking about something that is pleasing to God.

THE RED X

When you have a damaging thought (or image) come to your mind, recognize it as worry or anxiety getting the best of you. Close your eyes and imagine drawing a big red X over the image in your mind. Then, imagine yourself breaking through the image and destroying it. Redirect your thoughts to focus on something better.

FIGHT

When you feel afraid and you start to worry, remember to use the FIGHT tool. You may feel a little silly at first, but talk out loud and remind yourself of God's truth. The more you use the FIGHT tool, the easier it will be for you to overcome worry.

W Work through your worry (step one)
O Overcome fear (step two)
R Reclaim your thoughts (step three)
R Release control (step four)
Y Your hope is in Jesus (step five)

Often, worry strikes us when we least expect it. I hope this acronym (WORRY) will help you remember the steps we have covered.

Remember, you must work through your worry. It will not magically disappear. This is a journey, and it takes prayer, effort, time, and energy to do the work. Make journaling a habit in your life to help you work through your worry.

Worry is rooted in fear. The starting point to overcoming worry is to first recognize your fears and know you can overcome them. When fear overtakes your heart and mind, God can give you the courage to face it head-on. Remember, fear is just a feeling and by itself, it has no power over you.

You can reclaim your thoughts by paying attention to your inner voice. You decide which thoughts take up residence in your mind. When fearful, anxious thoughts creep in, remember the analogy of the spider and kick those thoughts out by changing the channel in your mind. Don't dwell on the "what ifs," instead, dwell on the things of God.

You are not in control of everything that happens in your life, but you are in control of how you respond to what happens. Release control by trusting in God. He is the potter, and you are the clay. He has a good plan in mind for your life. Trust in Him when trouble comes.

Hope is powerful, and your hope is in Jesus, alone. Pain, heartache, brokenness, and suffering are only temporary. Those feelings will not last forever. Worry will cause your perspective to be blurry. Put on your lens of hope as you walk through difficult times. Heaven is real and when we belong to Jesus, one day we will be with God, forever.

Practicing these five steps and utilizing the tools I outlined in Step Two was instrumental for me in overcoming worry. My nervous system was stuck in overdrive and the Cycle of Worry was spinning out of control, but as I began using those steps and tools, my mind and body felt calmer. My nervous system was encouraged to release feel-good, calming hormones and chemicals. This helped me cope.

Over time, I found more ways to improve my well-being and peace of mind when worry tried to sneak in. Life is stressful and worry comes and goes. We need to establish healthy habits to prevent worry from becoming excessive. When we support and encourage our nervous systems, we help prevent worry from taking over our thought lives. Many of the tips and suggestions below have helped me.

- Finding a trusted healthcare provider
- Checking your bloodwork and labs
- Improving your sleep
- Improving your diet
- Increasing mild to moderate exercise
- Gentle physical touch (back scratch, foot rub, etc.)
- Regular massages
- Listening to calming music
- Spending time outdoors - more sunshine
- Supplements and medication

FINDING A TRUSTED HEALTHCARE PROVIDER

It is important for you to find a healthcare provider you can talk to about how you feel. If you do not have a provider you can trust, pray and ask God to lead you to the right person. Your healthcare provider can work with you to help you overcome your struggle with worry.

BLOOD TEST/LABS

Assessing your overall health is a good place to start when you feel overly worried or anxious. A blood test is a common lab test where a small amount of blood is taken to assess organ function and certain medical conditions. When you feel anxious for a lengthy amount of time, ask your healthcare provider if they think having a blood test could be helpful. Not everyone who struggles with anxiety needs this type of testing, but it can be helpful in some cases. Lab values that come back outside of the normal range provide valuable feedback on how your organs are working and if there are any underlying conditions that need to be addressed.

There are several medical conditions that mimic symptoms of anxiety. For example, you can have thyroid issues that cause you to feel nervous, irritable, and restless. Someone who has diabetes may experience low blood glucose levels (blood sugar) that cause shakiness, sweatiness, and an increased heart rate. Electrolyte imbalances, respiratory conditions, asthma, gastrointestinal conditions, and heart issues can also cause symptoms that mimic anxiety.

After my personal illness, a blood test revealed that I had lower levels of magnesium in my body. Magnesium is an electrolyte that plays a crucial role in regulating nerve and muscle function. It also aids in blood glucose control and blood pressure. At the suggestion of my physician, I began taking a magnesium supplement and I experienced great benefits in how I felt.

Talk with your primary healthcare provider to see if having

labwork done is right for you. It may provide useful information that could improve your overall physical health.

SLEEP

One way anxiety robbed me of joy was by robbing me of restful sleep. Restful sleep can be described as sleep that comes naturally, is uninterrupted, and lasts at least seven hours. Without restful sleep, your body struggles to function effectively. Studies show that the lack of restful sleep affects multiple areas of your life including your mood and metabolism.

One problem with worry is that it often rears its ugly head at bedtime. When things are quiet and dark, the "what ifs" come flooding into our minds. We worry about what might happen and all of the potential bad things that may come to us...and then we worry about what time it is and how much sleep we will get if we fall asleep right now...and then when we don't fall asleep, we worry about how much less sleep we are getting...does any of this sound familiar to you?

There is a term used that evaluates our approach to sleep. It is called sleep hygiene. Sleep hygiene is one of the keys to achieving restful sleep. Healthy sleep hygiene means we implement a routine into our lives that promotes consistent, uninterrupted sleep. It includes two main things:

- The habits you instill before bed
- What type of environment you are sleeping in

How is your sleep hygiene? Your sleep routine should be consistent and your sleeping environment should be one that is peaceful, soothing, and inviting. It should encourage consistent, uninterrupted sleep. It is important to evaluate your own personal sleep hygiene and the good news is, you can implement changes to greatly improve your sleep hygiene.

When I struggled with worry and anxiety, my sleep was affected to a level that altered my life (in a negative way). I had taken for granted the ability I had to fall asleep easily and stay asleep. I had never had issues with sleeping. I have always loved to sleep! In high school, I could sleep until noon with no problem! When worry and anxiety invaded my life, it was like I had forgotten how to fall asleep and stay asleep. My anxious thoughts invaded my mind to the point that I could not fall asleep.

If you are struggling with sleep, the importance of a sleep schedule cannot be overstated. Implementing a relaxing pre-bed routine is an important piece of healthy sleep hygiene. How you prepare for sleep can determine how easily you will fall asleep and how well you will sleep. Below are a few suggestions you can use to help improve your sleep.

- Have a bedtime routine and stick to it: Follow the same routine, in order, every night. This includes things like taking a bath first, then brushing your teeth, then putting on your pajamas, etc. Implement a routine that works for you. As you stick to the same order and routine, you are signaling to your brain that it is bedtime and that sleep is near.

- Take time to wind down before bed: What makes you feel relaxed? Is it a warm bath? Is it a glass of warm milk? Maybe it's reading a book or listening to calming music. Whatever calms you, implement that into your bedtime routine. Give yourself 30 minutes to wind down each night before turning off the light to go to sleep.

- Keep your lights dim as you unwind: Your body makes melatonin (a hormone that helps you sleep). Melatonin is produced more when the lights are dimmer. Bright lights prevent melatonin from being produced at a healthy level for sleep.

- Turn off your electronics: Cell phones, tablets, televisions, and computers stimulate your brain to stay awake. They also emit blue light which can decrease melatonin levels. As you are winding down in the evening, turn off your electronics 30 minutes to one hour before bed. This signals to your mind that you are preparing to sleep.

- Create a relaxing, cooler, bedroom environment: Fresh sheets, a comfy pillow, blankets and even adding a relaxing fragrance in the air may help you feel calm and joyful. This invites sleep.

- Use relaxation methods that help you feel calm and relaxed: Reading my Bible before bed and spending time in prayer have been game changers for me as I rest and relax my anxious mind. Putting yourself in the right mindset is important for healthy sleep hygiene.

- Use white noise to drown out noises in your home: This tip may not work for everyone, especially if you have a baby or small children at home, but using white noise has been instrumental for me when it comes to being able to fall asleep easily. When you struggle with sleep, you hear every little noise in your house. Using a white noise app on your phone or tablet can help cancel out the background noises in your house so you can fall asleep easier.

- Block out any light: Your mind needs a dark space to sleep well. Have curtains or blinds on your bedroom windows to block out any light. You may want to wear an eye mask to help block out light.

- Use your bed for sleeping and intimacy only: Some people find that if they use their bed for any activity besides sleep or intimacy with their spouse, it inhibits their ability to sleep. If you play games on your electronic devices while you lie in bed, try playing those games on the couch or in another part of your house. This may signal to your brain that when you get into bed, it is time for sleep.

DIET AND EXERCISE/MOVEMENT

Although eating a proper diet and increasing physical activity in our lives do not cure worry or anxiety, they are both important pieces to our overall health. Our diets fuel our bodies, and by examining what we eat, we learn ways to improve the fuel we give our bodies. It's no secret that adding more fruits and vegetables into our diets is healthy for our minds and bodies. Adding more whole foods to our diets and decreasing caffeine consumption can also help with stress levels and improve how we feel.

You may wonder how important exercise is in helping with stress and anxiety. Studies show that people with low rates of physical movement in their lives are over 75% more likely to have anxiety and/or depression. That's a big percentage! Moving your body is very important because it reduces the levels of stress hormones and chemicals. It also increases the chemicals in your brain that elevate your mood and help with pain. Exercise helps clear our minds and decreases the "what if" thoughts we have when we worry. Moving our bodies is an essential part of a healthy lifestyle.

It is easy to list out the benefits of physical activity, but if you do not already have a regular exercise routine, it can be difficult to know where to start. When I need to implement a change into my life, I try to remember that life is about habits. Our daily habits define so much of who we are. If you want to lower your stress hormones, then look for ways you can move your body, more. Once you decide to increase your daily physical activity, it will become easier and easier for you to stick with it! Some easy ways to get started is to look for ways to add more physical activity into your normal routine.

- Take the stairs instead of the elevator.
- Park farther away from work or a store.
- Increase your speed of walking during normal activities.
- Instead of a sit-down meeting, schedule a "walking" meeting with a coworker. Walk outside to soak in more sunshine and Vitamin D.
- Invite a friend to be your walking buddy.
- Keep up with how many steps you take each day (use an app or a watch that counts your steps).

If you want to begin a more intentional exercise plan, strive to spend 20 to 40 minutes of walking briskly most days of the week. Walking is a great way to decrease stress and improve your mood. The goal is to safely increase your heart rate, so you want to move faster than your normal walking speed. As you work to decrease stress in your body, consider adding strength training to your regimen. Lightweights help develop muscle tone and aid in stress management. There are many exercises you can do at home to help build muscle tone and decrease stress. Many people also find great benefits from doing stretching exercises a few times each week. Stretching is very beneficial for our bodies. It builds muscle tone, keeps muscles flexible, and can improve the range of motion in our joints. When we do not stretch, our muscles become tight and are more prone to injury.

Take a few minutes and write down ways you can improve your diet and add exercise to your daily habits. Be specific and write down a start date to implement these changes.

Ways I can improve my diet:

_____

_____

_____

_____

_____

_____

_____

Ways I can add more physical activity into my daily habits:

_____

_____

_____

_____

_____

_____

_____

MEDICATION

As a Christ-centered pharmacist, I want to share with you my thoughts about the use of medication when it comes to worry and anxiety. I realize people hold strong opinions when it comes to taking medication, so this section may be a little uncomfortable for some people. Not everyone is in favor of taking medication to help with anxiety, and that is okay. I hope you will keep reading as I explain my thoughts and expertise in this area.

I am not someone who believes there is a pill for every ailment. Often, lifestyle changes can be used to correct medical issues, but sometimes, lifestyle changes are not enough. I am grateful to live in a country where I have access to medications. God has allowed scientists to develop medications and they are used every day to save lives.

Medicines are not a new concept. Throughout history, natural plants and other substances have been used to heal physical ailments. It is interesting when we look in our Bibles, we see medicines were used then to heal illnesses, too.

God can heal people in any way He chooses. He has the power to heal us miraculously without medicine, and He has the power to use medicines to heal our bodies. Several times in the Bible, we see scripture that references a medicinal plant or substance that brought about healing for people.

And on the banks, on both sides of the river, there will grow all kinds of trees for food. Their leaves will not wither, nor their fruit fail, but they will bear fresh fruit every month, because the water for them flows from the sanctuary. Their fruit will be for food, and their leaves for healing.
~Ezekiel 47:12

Is there no balm in Gilead? Is there no physician there?
Why then is there no healing for the wound of my people?
~Jeremiah 8:22

Get balm for her pain; perhaps she can be healed.
~Jeremiah 51:8b

Now Isaiah had said, "Let them take a cake of figs
and apply it to the boil, that he may recover."
~Isaiah 38:21

I have spent a significant amount of my career studying and practicing pharmacy and teaching pharmacy students. Although the pharmaceutical industry has its blemishes, I believe God gave mankind the intellect to discover Him through science. He has allowed scientists to develop medications that aid in healing and comfort. Maybe you have benefited from using medication for an illness in your life.

My nephew was diagnosed with Type 1 diabetes at the young age of five. Without injecting insulin into his body every day, he would die. I am grateful to scientists who researched and developed insulin.

My brother-in-law had a major medical illness and was the recipient of a liver transplant that saved his life. He had to take medications to prevent his body from rejecting his new liver. I am grateful for the scientists who researched and developed these life-giving anti-rejection medicines.

Medication can also help people who experience excessive worry and anxiety. As the Cycle of Worry spins out of control, brain chemicals and hormones become unbalanced. This can lead to chronic anxiety that can drastically affect someone's quality of life. For many people, medication can help correct these imbalances. When someone's nervous system is in hyperdrive, medicine is a tool that may encourage and support their nervous system. Medications often "take the edge off" for people so they feel mentally stronger and physically calmer to work through their worry and anxiety. Medication is designed to bring balance to the central nervous system which may help someone cope with the anxiety they are experiencing. It is often used as a bridge between feeling trapped in worry and anxiety and finding a mindset of peace.

There is no one size fits all medication plan for worry and anxiety. For some people, medication does not work at all. Other times a person finds benefit from taking medication for a short period of time, and some people need medication for a much longer period of time.

There are several classes of medications used to help with anxiety. Anti-anxiety medications and antidepressant medications are two examples commonly used. There are also medications that are used to help with sleep and many people find them beneficial. It is important to keep in mind there are side effects and drug interactions that come into play. Also, it may take some time to find the right medication. Although one medication may not work for someone, another medication may. If you are prescribed medication for your anxiety, it is important to be patient and give it time to work. It can take up to eight weeks before you feel the full effects.

The decision to use medication for excessive worry or anxiety should be thoughtfully and prayerfully considered. If you feel you are in a more serious place with worry or anxiety, or if you are having thoughts of self-harm, please talk openly with your healthcare provider. With a careful review of your overall medical history, you and your healthcare provider can work together to find the best plan of action. If you choose to explore medication for excessive worry or anxiety, remember to pray and ask God to guide you down the best path. Ask Him to give you wisdom as you make this important decision.

RELATIONSHIPS

God designed us to have community with one another. We need healthy, happy relationships with other people. From the beginning of human life, God showed us that we need one another.

> *The LORD God said, "It is not good for the man to be*
> *alone. I will make a helper suitable for him."*
> *~Genesis 2:18*

Medical studies show that having healthy relationships is the biggest predictor of living a happy life. Good social relationships are also connected to living a longer life and having better health. When healthy relationships are nonexistent in a person's life or when relationships are toxic, feelings of worry, anxiety, and loneliness emerge. When people who are close to us bring out the worst in us, we need to pay attention to how those relationships affect our state of mind. We need to pray. We need to set healthy boundaries and expectations. We may need to talk to a counselor.

Not everyone has a happy, healthy marriage. Not everyone has a happy, healthy work environment. Not everyone has a supportive family that encourages them through the ups and downs of life. Unhealthy relationships can cause major stress in our lives. If you find yourself in a relationship that is causing you to worry excessively, first talk to God about it. Ask Him for help. Study your Bible and ask God to give you wisdom. Ask Him to help you handle this situation in a way that pleases Him. Next, talk to someone you trust; a friend, a pastor, or a Christian counselor. Use your journal and write down how you feel. Remember to use the strategies we've covered in this book to manage your stress and worry.

Relationships are hard and they take work. I've learned when two people mutually agree to work on their unhealthy relationship there is hope to make that relationship better. I have witnessed it firsthand. It does take time, energy, and work, but it is worth the effort to save the relationship. Unfortunately, sometimes both people in the unhealthy relationship are not willing to work through things, and the relationship does not improve. In these situations, life becomes very stressful. One person may want to save the relationship but the other person is not willing to work on things. If this is a situation you find yourself in, depending on the nature of your relationship, you will have some tough decisions to make. If this unhealthy relationship is with a friend or a distant family member, you may need to put up emotional boundaries and love this person from a distance. If this relationship is with your husband, child, or close family member, the next step becomes more complicated. You may benefit from talking to a Christian counselor or pastor to help you navigate the next steps. Relationships can be taxing, but be determined not to give up! Keep praying! Keep seeking God's will in this relationship.

People are messy. No one is perfect. In any relationship, it is important we examine our own flaws and insecurities. We need to pray and search our hearts to see what we can do to exemplify Jesus in the relationship. If an unhealthy relationship is causing you excessive worry, stress, or anxiety, take steps to improve how you interact with this person. Here are a few suggestions you may find helpful:

- Pray for the person who is causing you to feel stressed.
- Go to the Word of God for guidance and listen for God's still, small voice to guide you.
- Pray before you discuss the problem with this person.
- Speak the truth (in love) to this person.
- Actively listen to their view of things.
- Show compassion, respect, and kindness.
- Never belittle this person or insult them.
- Use "I" statements (not "You" statements):
  - Do say: "I want our relationship to be better."
  - Do say: "I feel _____ when this happens."
  - Don't say: "You always make me feel..."
- When you feel angry during a discussion, don't yell or lash out. Instead, take a few deep breaths before you speak.
- It is okay to step away from the conversation if emotions become too intense.

Remember, friend, God knows your heart. He knows the depths of your pain. It is not good for you to bottle up how you feel. It is therapeutic for you to *get out* your feelings in the right way. Find time to be alone with God and tell Him how you feel. He wants you to come to Him and pour out your heart. Pray and keep praying. Study your Bible. Put your trust in God and know He has the power to help you. He loves you. He sees you. He is with you.

Final Thoughts

A NOTE OF ENCOURAGEMENT

My friend, I am so thankful you and I have been on this journey together to overcome worry. I hope your heart is encouraged as you remember God desires for you to experience His joy and His peace! He has a good plan for your life, and He does not want you to miss it.

Remember - the transformation of your life begins with the renewing of your mind. Keep your thoughts aligned with God's Word and His desires for you. Keep your eyes on Him as you walk your life's journey. Keep your heart open to what He reveals to you, and be determined to fight back against the stronghold worry has on your life.

You have tools, strategies, and tips you can use to overcome excessive worry. Mostly, you have a loving heavenly Father who wants to help you! Rely on Him and put your trust in Him. You can be courageous by facing your fears head-on. Courage is not the absence of fear, courage is moving forward in spite of fear.

There are some things you cannot control in life, but you are in control of many things, including these:

- what you think about
- your attitude
- your prayer life
- your walk with God
- your words
- your actions
- your choices
- your responses
- how you manage your thoughts
- how you manage your feelings
- how you manage your relationships
- how you take care of yourself

Satan wants you to feel hopeless and helpless. He will try to convince you there is no way out of the darkness you feel. He will lie to you and try to confuse you about what you know is true. Do not believe his lies. There is a way out of the darkness you feel - it's through trusting in Jesus who is the light of the world.

When Jesus spoke again to the people, he said,
"I am the light of the world. Whoever follows me will
never walk in darkness but will have the light of life."
~John 8:12

Worry is a joy-stealer, relationship-breaker, and life-thief. When it invades your life, you cannot jump over it, crawl around it or swim under it. You must walk through it, but you can walk through it with strength and courage because you are not alone. Jesus is with you!

You can live a joy-filled life even when life is hard. Real joy is found through a personal relationship with Jesus. He is the way, the truth, and the life. He left Heaven and came to Earth to give you life, and He wants you to have life in all its fullness!

The thief comes only to steal and kill and destroy; I have
come that they may have life, and have it to the full.
~John 10:10

Grateful for you!
~Dr. Joy

Scriptures to help with worry

Psalm 55:22

Matthew 11:28-30

John 14:27

Romans 8:28

Philippians 4:6-7

Colossians 3:15

2 Thessalonians 3:16

Look up each of the scriptures above and write a few of them on sticky notes. Place those sticky notes in prominent areas of your home or office area so you see them each day. Read them out loud and fill up your mind with God's truth!

Scriptures to fight fear

Deuteronomy 31:6

Psalm 23:4

Psalm 27:1

Psalm 46:1

Psalm 56:3

Psalm 94:19

Psalm 118:6-7

Isaiah 41:10

Matthew 6:25-34

Mark 5:36

1 Peter 5:7

Look up each of the scriptures above and write a few of them on sticky notes. Place those sticky notes in prominent areas of your home or office area so you see them each day. Read them out loud and fill up your mind with God's truth!

Scriptures about joy

Nehemiah 8:10

Psalm 30:5

Proverbs 17:22

Romans 12:12

Philippians 4:4

Hebrews 12:2

James 1:2

John 16:22

Look up each of the scriptures above and write a few of them on sticky notes. Place those sticky notes in prominent areas of your home or office area so you see them each day. Read them out loud and fill up your mind with God's truth!

Find other Joytime journals and books on Amazon!

Open your phone camera app and point it at this QR Code. Tap the link that pops up. You can also write a review of this book at this link.

31 DEVOTIONS
FOR WOMEN

Dr. Joy Greene

Joytime

BIBLE STUDY JOURNAL

Printed in Great Britain
by Amazon

26051271R00106